Richard Triggs

✦ Author of *Uncover the Hidden Job Market* ✦

WINNING
THE WAR FOR
TALENT

How to attract and retain top performers

A catalogue entry for this book is available from the National Library of Australia.

ISBN: 978-1-923007-80-2

Printed in Australia by Pegasus Media & Logistics
Book production and text design by Publish Central
Cover design by Julia Kuris

The paper this book is printed on is certified as environmentally friendly.

Disclaimer

Contents

Firstly, a very big thank you to ...

Although I am the author of this book, so much of the information I have presented comes from the tremendous mentors, bosses and coaches I have been fortunate to have during my career. So in no particular order, with the absolute deepest gratitude, thank you to Colin Clerke, Rex Urwin and Andrew Griffiths for your fantastic support over the years. You are all amazing coaches and friends, and I have benefitted so much from working with you.

Thank you to Adrian Luus for coming into my life a few years ago, working with me as a psychotherapist and subsequently training me also. Adrian, his wife Bonita and son Shane, and the extended Sacred Healing community, have become so important to me, and I look forward to remaining great friends for the rest of our lives.

Thank you to two amazing bosses in particular that I learned so much from, Peter King and Bruce Davidson. What I learned from both of you in relation to leadership has served me so well in my career.

Thank you to Lou Adler, who I have referenced many times in this book for his recruitment genius. The training I received from you so many years ago in performance-based hiring remains my preferred methodology and the foundation of Arete Executive's success.

Thank you to my amazing team at Arete Executive. I am so proud to work with such skilled professionals on a daily basis, and of the fantastic work we do together, helping others and ourselves realise our full potential.

And of course, thank you finally to my beautiful children Archie and Tallulah, my mum Ruth, and also to Fiona for your love and support.

Introduction

Where Buddha meets Bill Gates

Welcome and congratulations

Writing a book is like inviting someone to come and live inside your head for a little while. Putting deeply personal thoughts into the world for people to read is quite daunting. So let me start by saying welcome to my mind. I hope that for however long you choose to hang out here you find it interesting, thought-provoking and hopefully a bit of fun too. And secondly, congratulations on picking up this book and investing time to learn new skills to enhance your own businesses, careers and lives in general. I know your time is very valuable, and I greatly appreciate that you are spending some of it with yours truly.

Let's chat about Sally and Mike for a little bit.

Sally is the CEO of a large professional services company. She loves her job, and her board loves her. Yet she is constantly feeling frustrated and anxious about her ability to meet the outcomes required by her key stakeholders. She seems to be working longer and longer hours just trying to get everything done. She desperately needs to grow her team, yet her HR department is producing underwhelming shortlists of candidates for mission-critical roles. Their excuse is that there's 'a war for talent' and good people are simply too hard to find.

Mike is a successful business owner who has seen his entrepreneurial idea rapidly grow into an exciting and dynamic company. He has a clear vision for the future; however, he's concerned about staff turnover and the constant stop/start distraction of having to replace employees. When he meets with other business owners, talk often goes to the 'great resignation' and the fact that employees, especially those of the younger generation, have no loyalty anymore.

Recruitment does not have to be a burden

Organisations live or die based on the quality of their people. You can provide the highest quality, most innovative and exciting products or services, but if you can't attract and retain top performers, your business is never going to achieve its full potential. Fundamental to leading any kind of organisation is the recruitment, performance management and retention of employees. There's simply no way around it unless you want to be a sole trader.

So why are many business leaders terrible at this most fundamental task? How many times have you heard someone say, 'if it wasn't for staff, my job would be easy'? You may even have said this yourself.

Don't you think it's time to invest in educating yourself and the hiring managers in your business to develop these skills? Wouldn't it be fantastic to actually view recruiting as a fun and exciting part of your job, rather than a burden? Imagine each member of your team being fully engaged and performing to their highest potential, both individually and collectively. Imagine being able to say with complete honesty, 'my job is easy, because of my fantastic staff'.

This book has been written with that exact outcome in mind. It provides a simple, practical methodology to hire and retain top performers. This book is for busy leaders who don't have time for convoluted and academic theories and models, they just want results.

A couple of elephants

Let's briefly address a couple of elephants in the room before we go any further.

Firstly, a lot of you will say, and believe, that because you have hired many people in your career (in some cases it could be hundreds), you know all there is to be learned about recruitment and retention through the 'school of hard knocks'. However, my favourite saying is 'the truth is the result'. If you still have hard-to-fill roles, or good people still leave your business, there is definitely more for you to learn and implement.

The second elephant in the room is that because you are so busy, and have far more urgent, mission-critical tasks to perform, you have delegated the role of recruitment to your HR team (or to third-party recruiters) and the role of retention to your line managers. After all, that's what they are paid for, right? Again, even if they have impeccable formal qualifications and extensive career experience, if you still have hard-to-fill roles, or good people still leave your business, as the ultimate leader (even if that is just for your division or department) it's your responsibility to get it right.

So who am I?

So who am I to write this book? Well, after a short-lived career following high school as an aspiring rock star (I toured Australia playing guitar in bands for four years), I went back to university and completed a Bachelor of Commerce degree, majoring in Marketing and Human Resources. I then worked in the building services industry in sales and then operational management roles. At 26, I took on my first leadership role with a team of approximately 100 staff, and by age 30 I was leading a team of over 750 people, dispersed all over Australia.

In 2002, while completing an Executive MBA, I decided I wanted a career change. I went to see a recruiter I had previously been a client of, who suggested I might actually enjoy a career in recruitment myself. The rest, as they say, is history. After working for the largest privately owned recruitment company in Queensland, including sitting on their board as an Executive Director, I started my own executive recruitment company, Arete Executive, in 2009. I would conservatively say we have placed over 2000 senior executives and board directors in roles throughout Australia.

I've also coached and mentored hundreds of CEOs and business owners in relation to their careers, recruitment and leadership through a variety of programmes, including my Sounding Board mastermind groups.

At the same time, I've always had a fascination with Eastern philosophy and personal and spiritual development. In my 30s I lived one weekend per month for four years in the largest community of Buddhist monks and nuns in the Southern Hemisphere, called the Chenrezig Institute. There I completed an extremely intense four-year course in Buddhism and actually at one stage considered becoming a monk. I've done many other retreats and courses over the years which I believe have given me some unique perspectives around business and leadership, which I'm going to share with you in this book. To steal a phrase from my very good friend and mentor Colin Clerke, it's like 'where Buddha meets Bill Gates'.

How to get the most out of this book

The purpose of this book is to educate you on how best to recruit for your business yourself. The book is divided into two parts. In the first part, focused on attracting top performers, you're going to learn how to:

- create and promote your personal brand and your organisation's brand as an Employer of Choice

- develop briefs to ensure you consistently recruit the right kind of people for your roles

- run a comprehensive campaign to source the very best performers, rather than just relying on responses to advertisements

- interview impeccably to ensure you are selecting the highest quality of talent

- best manage the offer process to secure new employees and avoid counteroffers.

In the second part, focused on retaining top performers, you're going to learn how to:

- understand the psychology of performance and what traits can both positively and negatively affect performance

- establish a culture of performance from the very top down

- onboard new employees into this culture from the very first day

- use a performance management framework, called the Preferred Reality model, to drive performance and accountability across individuals, teams, other stakeholders and yourself.

By the time you have finished reading, I guarantee that no matter your starting point, you will have significantly improved your game in relation to hiring and leading high-performance employees. You will be positively excited about your next hiring exercise. Through implementing the performance management tools you'll learn about in this book, your existing team will immediately become more motivated and results driven. Most importantly, you'll have extra time to invest in more strategic tasks and achieve the work/life balance you have always dreamed of.

The best way to maximise the effectiveness of this book is to read it from cover to cover the first time. The book follows a specific structure, and it will make the most sense if you do so, as each chapter builds on the previous ones. However, once you have done so, you can easily dip back into the book and read the relevant chapter for the task or challenge you are facing at that particular time, as each part is broken down into task-specific chapters that you can refresh yourself about as required. Also, make sure you have your management team read this book as well, so you have a common language to utilise to assist and support each other.

Let's have some fun and enjoy spending this time together. Time spent reading this book is time you could have spent on other work-related tasks, or with family and friends. So once again, I honour and respect my obligation to deliver great value, to stimulate and sometimes challenge your thinking, and to leave you feeling delighted you invested your valuable time in this book.

I can't wait to see you on the other side.

The war for talent, the great resignation and other myths

At the time of writing, the world is very much at the tail end of the Covid-19 pandemic. Business optimism is high (regardless of what you hear in the media), organisations are growing, and candidates are back to being active in the market and looking for new opportunities.

There has definitely been a cultural shift in the way people are looking at their careers and the way they wish to be engaged with their employers. Working from home, working part time, telecommuting and contracting versus permanent employment are not new phenomena. However, the zeitgeist has definitely changed as more and more people want these alternate arrangements rather than the traditional Monday-to-Friday, nine-to-five employment model.

These trends were definitely happening pre-Covid, especially with improving internet speed and availability, virtual meetings over Zoom and Teams, and other technology. It's just that the pandemic and resulting lockdowns and travel restrictions greatly accelerated candidates' desire for change. However, the fundamental recruiting environment remains largely the same as it was 20 years ago when I first started my recruitment career, especially the excuses for poor hiring and retention, so let's dispel two of these right from the get-go.

Myth: the war for talent

When I first started working in the recruitment industry in 2002, I joined TMP Worldwide (now known as Hudson). At the time they were the biggest recruitment company in the world, and I was excited about joining such a prestigious brand. I clearly remember, in my very first days of induction, being introduced to this term of doom and gloom, 'the war for talent', designed to spread fear among employers and to lower their expectations regarding the quality of candidates they would see on a shortlist presented by us. It's not dissimilar to a real estate agent manipulating homeowners into accepting a lower price for their house, because 'it's a buyer's market out there' so the owner should be grateful to receive an offer at all.

It amazed me that recruiters basically sold a service by pre-emptively conditioning employers to be underwhelmed. More importantly, that's exactly the level of service they then delivered. On the other hand, I believed (and still do) that as recruitment professionals, we must be able to guarantee to deliver outstanding shortlists, which requires a headhunting approach. In fact, at the time of writing this book, at my firm Arete Executive, unless we deliver a shortlist within 20 working days that our client is delighted to interview, we offer to refund our client their retainer. If we say we can deliver the result, we should hold the risk of non-performance.

It's 20 years later and I still hear about the 'war for talent' on an almost daily basis, from CEOs and business owners, HR managers and internal and external recruiters. Quite frankly, it's a load of BS and the fact that it is perpetuated is just an indication of how dumb and lazy most people charged with recruitment are. Rather than working harder and smarter to attract outstanding candidates, it's so much easier to just blame the market and accept mediocrity.

Let me give you a couple of examples. Earlier this year my recruitment company was engaged by one of the biggest mining companies in the world to recruit for them an HR manager in regional Australia (I won't tell you their name, however if you think about the top three Australian global mining companies, it's definitely one of them.)

Now this particular mining company had this role vacant for close to eight months, and the fact it remained vacant was causing a lot of distress to the line manager as it was significantly impacting their ability to do their job and deliver results well. Yet the head of internal recruitment, who was responsible for finding candidates and filling the role, had not delivered on what was a fairly simple brief, even after such a long period. The excuse – 'it's a war for talent' – was there were no suitable candidates in the region, or who wanted to move to the region. They had essentially given up, while still paying lip service to some continued sourcing activity taking place.

Eventually, the line manager was given permission to engage us to deliver a suitable shortlist, which we were able to do in less than two weeks, that resulted in a very fast and successful placement. Why were we able to get such an immediate and positive result? Because unlike the internal recruiter who simply placed a bland and uninspiring advertisement on Seek and sent a few lacklustre InMails on LinkedIn, we undertook a comprehensive sourcing strategy that left no stone unturned.

This is what I am going to teach you how to do in this book.

My second example. Recently I ran a 'Lunch and Learn' event on Zoom, talking to business owners and CEOs about how to recruit top talent. One particular CEO was unable to attend and asked if his Head of HR and Head of Recruitment could attend in his place. His business is a privately owned engineering company.

I started the session by asking each attendee to describe their current recruitment challenges; what was 'the pebble in their shoe?', or what was 'keeping them awake at night?' The two HR attendees from this engineering firm explained that they currently had over 40 vacancies, the quality of their advertisement response was underwhelming, plus most good applicants pulled out of the process before they even attended their first interview.

Through asking some probing questions it became obvious that they were not bothering to take quality briefs from the hiring manager, they were writing very boring job advertisements, they were not making themselves available to speak to potential applicants, and it was often over three weeks between someone making an application and an interview being arranged. Plus they were doing zero headhunting.

It's no wonder their results were so poor. And yet here is a CEO who is probably paying combined salaries of over $250k to employ these two HR 'specialists', he has over 40 current vacancies and no doubt he is extremely frustrated and concerned about his firm's ability to deliver for their clients and other stakeholders. Interestingly, when I offered to speak further with these two HR staff and offer additional advice, neither of them returned my phone calls or emails (which is a pretty typical reaction).

In the immortal words of Jerry Ziesmer in *Apocalypse Now*, if I was their CEO I would immediately 'terminate with extreme prejudice' (what a great line from an awesome movie). There is absolutely no excuse for what was obviously lazy and inept performance from the

HR team. Yet they continue to remain employed and continue to offer the same BS excuse to their boss, 'Sorry dude, it's just that there's a war for talent'. Give me a freaking break!

So let's get one thing clear – there is no war for talent, there never has been and if you are being duped into believing this then do so at your own peril. There are simple, proven and consistently successful recruitment strategies that allow some companies to recruit easily; and on the other side of the coin, there are lazy and incompetent people who are wasting your time and money by being crap at their jobs.

The good news is I am going to teach you the right way to recruit in this book, so you will accept no further excuses in the future.

You are learning a new superpower!

Myth: the great resignation

How many times have you heard this phrase in the last couple of years, especially in our post-Covid world: 'It's not my fault we can't retain people – it's the great resignation'? It's as if everyone drank the Kool-Aid while working from home, and woke up hating their boss, hating their employer, hating their profession, and all wanting to quit and join the circus.

'Especially the younger generation, who want the world and show no loyalty to their current employer,' complains the older senior executive while talking to me about looking for a new job and an extra $100k. Ahhh, the joys of hypocrisy.

In 2010, a global poll conducted by Gallup uncovered that of the world's one billion full-time workers, only 15 per cent of people were engaged at work. That means an astronomical 85 per cent of people were unhappy in their jobs.

The average professional job tenure in Australia from 2000 to 2022 has consistently sat at around 3.0 to 3.5 years. This means that people change employers roughly every three years. A recent PwC report on the 'great resignation', 'What Workers Want: How to win the war on talent', found that 38 per cent of Australian workers intend to leave their current employer during the next 12 months. Which is, guess what? A tenure of about 3.0 to 3.5 years. So the more things change, the more they stay the same.

There is no great resignation, it's just media doom and gloom being fed by consultants trying to sell more snake oil (anyone remember Y2K?).

My simple explanation is this. During Covid there were a lot of people who wanted to change jobs, however chose not to do so because they felt the risk of change at that time was too high. 'What if I change jobs and then get Covid, but don't have any accrued sick leave or annual leave?' Or, 'What if I change jobs and then my new employer is negatively impacted by Covid, and I end up being made redundant?'

So they stayed in jobs longer than they would have normally because it was a safe harbour in a storm. Now that Covid is largely behind us, these people are resigning for new opportunities. Covid was just a bottleneck and now the employment market has returned to normal. The statistics prove this.

I can honestly say I have not had a single regrettable loss from my business in over five years. Likewise, I know countless CEOs and business owners who have been able to retain all their top performers both during and post Covid. They have invested time and money into building their brands as Employers of Choice, and in maintaining a performance-based culture that encourages and rewards exceptional individual and team performance.

Just like the war for talent, the great resignation is a crappy excuse for poor leadership. The great news is that you are going to learn how to build and maintain a culture to not only attract high performers to your businesses, but also to retain them for much longer than industry averages.

Other myths and clichés

There are so many other myths around recruitment, leadership and retention that I could write a whole book on this subject.

Then there are the clichés that seem to be repeated in every business book, such as, 'strategy eats culture for breakfast' (Peter Drucker), or 'start with why' (Simon Sinek), or even 'courage over comfort' (Brené Brown). In their time, these ideas were thought-provoking and challenged some old business paradigms, but they just seem a bit naff now through endless regurgitation (a bit like Rick Astley's *Never Gonna Give You Up* – thank you *Ted Lasso* for being such an awesome TV show).

How about we just learn some simple tools and then go out and kick some butt?

Part I

Attracting top performers

As I mentioned at the beginning of this book, this first part will focus on hiring excellence (both being excellent at hiring and hiring excellent people – nice play on words, huh?). We will begin by addressing the question of whether you should do it yourself or engage a third-party recruitment company (spoiler alert: it depends) and also when you should start your hiring process.

Each stage will follow nicely from the one before, so you can just relax and 'follow the bouncing ball' (this saying apparently came from the original version of karaoke in movie theatres).

By the end of this part, you should be really clear on what a great recruitment process looks like. Whether you choose to do it yourself or delegate internally or externally, you will be far more confident that you will consistently end up with superior shortlists and hire fantastic people.

Chapter 1

To be, or not to be (the recruiter of your vacancy)?

Before I get into the pros and cons of using a recruitment agency versus managing your recruiting yourself, I thought I should clear the air about something that may be on your mind. Obviously, I own an executive recruitment agency and so (obviously) it's in my interest to be promoting the use of a recruitment company, and especially my company, all the time. However, I actually believe there are strong arguments for recruiting roles yourself, at least some of the time, and this book is written as a guide for how you (or your team) can recruit roles successfully rather than relying on external recruitment agencies.

So you can relax, no longer worrying about whether this book is just a really long sales brochure for Arete Executive.[1]

---

1   That said, of course if we can be of assistance, I'd love to see how we can help you.

Using a recruitment agency

Let me be blunt: **I wouldn't trust most recruiters to collect my mail**, let alone recruit staff for my business. Believe it or not, there are actually recruitment companies that specialise in recruiting recruitment consultants for recruitment companies (that's a bit of a tongue twister, so you might have to reread that sentence a couple of times). We call these 'rec-to-recs'. When I first joined the recruitment industry, I thought that rec-to-recs would have to be the best of the best, however direct experience has taught me most are just as useless as most regular recruiters, with all the same issues and headaches you have no doubt faced on many occasions personally, both as an employer and as a candidate.

I've heard all the stories and every possible complaint from employers about dealing with recruitment consultants, literally hundreds of times. Nothing you could tell me about your poor experiences would shock me; in fact, I'm sure I could tell you many stories that sound so implausible you'd be certain I was making it up (I've included a few in this book). For an industry that literally 'sells' people to other people, the general level of customer service and care is appalling.

The potential pitfalls of recruitment agencies

Unlike almost every other type of professional services industry, the recruitment industry requires no professional qualifications, has no barriers to entry and there are virtually no regulations. Literally any idiot could print a business card saying they are a recruitment consultant, and away they go. Prior to the Global Financial Crisis in 2008–09, in Brisbane alone there were over 600 registered recruitment companies. Although that number contracted during the GFC, and no doubt also during Covid, there are still new recruitment companies popping up on almost a weekly basis.

It is not uncommon for HR Managers to receive up to 40 cold calls per week from recruitment consultants asking to meet and/or pitch candidates. It's amazing how many of the recruitment consultants are mid-20s English backpackers who are now the new (pick the industry specialisation) expert at (pick the recruitment company – you know which ones I'm speaking about).

Believe it or not, **the recruitment industry generally has higher than 70 per cent annual staff turnover**. Approximately 90 per cent of people who join the recruitment industry leave within two years, never to return. Why is this, you ask? Because what generally happens is that a lawyer (for example – you can pick any profession here) becomes jaded with being a lawyer and is looking to try a new career. They go to see a recruitment company, who sells them on the amazing career they would have as a recruitment consultant (this is exactly what happened to me). Not only will they 'change people's lives by helping them achieve their dream jobs', companies also 'blue sky' them with how much money (commission) they will make.

So this lawyer becomes a recruitment consultant and quickly realises that mostly it's just a glorified sales job, with onerous KPIs and underwhelming leadership. After grinding out their 50 marketing calls a week for a few months (which is why the poor HR Manager is getting up to 40 unsolicited calls a week), they throw up their hands and typically return to the industry they had been desperate to leave not so long ago. Suddenly being a lawyer and charging in six-minute increments doesn't seem so bad after all (or an engineer, accountant, or whatever).

When I took my first job as a recruitment consultant, I was stunned that within the first 12 weeks, 14 of my colleagues resigned. Why did I stick it out? Because I love people and I love to sell. I had come from a strong KPI-driven sales environment, so this was nothing new to me. Plus, because I had previously been a senior executive and had just completed an MBA, I found it easy to build rapport and trust with my clients.

The other thing I realised within 12 weeks was that **if I wanted to be better than 9 out of 10 recruiters, I only needed to do one thing – return people's phone calls.** To this day, I am regularly told by people, including CEOs of some of the country's largest companies, that they simply can't get a call or email returned. (I had another one of these calls literally this morning.) It amazes me how many of my competitors pay lip service to 'today's candidate is tomorrow's client' yet can't even do something as simple as return a phone call.

Note that I said I wouldn't trust *most* recruiters to collect my mail, I didn't say *all* recruiters. Like any profession, there are some great recruitment consultants out there who are professional, courteous and can legitimately act as a trusted advisor (I would hope most people consider me and my team in this light). While it can be frustrating dealing with the vast majority of recruiters, when you find a good one (or preferably a few good ones), they can make your life a lot easier.

What's another reason you *wouldn't* use a recruitment agency? Using recruitment consultants is not dissimilar to paying for parking. When you are driving into the city for an important meeting, often you need to pay a hefty fee to use a centrally located parking facility. Nobody excitedly says, 'Wow, I just paid $80 to park my car for two hours, what an awesome investment!' Parking is a regrettable spend. You're in a hurry, and you appreciate the convenience of being able to park close to your appointment, but you certainly aren't excited about the fee.

Likewise paying for a third-party recruitment consultant to present candidates for your vacancy. Let's assume a mining company wants to hire a new CFO, and the salary is $300,000 per annum. A tier-one global search company could charge between 30 and 40 per cent of the salary for managing this assignment. For the sake of this illustration, let's say they use a local provider who offers to do the work for 20 per cent of the package, or $60,000 (20 per cent of $300k).

Now $60k in anyone's language is a lot of money. No employer is excited about paying this (it's a regrettable spend), however in the past they were obliged to because the recruitment consultant who specialises in identifying and placing CFOs has the database of candidates, and the employer wants access to these candidates. Your typical employer does not perceive that the recruitment consultant adds much, if any, value to the process. In fact, many employers regard recruitment consultants in the same light as used car salespeople – simply 'body shoppers'.

The situation now is very different. Probably 95 per cent of white-collar professionals have a LinkedIn profile, including CFOs. So the mining company says to their $80k per annum internal recruitment resource (often an early-career HR graduate or an external recruiter who has gone in-house to avoid the pressures of sales targets), 'Mary, we want you to find the details of every CFO at every ASX-listed mining company based in Brisbane. Preferably CPA qualified, preferably 15-plus years' experience, preferably having worked for one of the major coal mining companies'.

In an ideal world, Mary jumps onto LinkedIn using her Recruiter license, and using a few keyword searches she can easily and very quickly compile the list. She then shows the profiles to her boss, they agree on which individuals to target, and the recruitment process begins. So instead of the mining company paying $60k for one placement, they can employ Mary for almost an entire year and get much greater bang for their buck.

So the poor old traditional recruiter is, in my opinion, dying a certain and unavoidable death, never to be resuscitated. Their entire value proposition has been eroded, because for the first time ever, through using LinkedIn, employers have direct access to their prospective candidate pool, easily and cheaply.

Just like MYOB and Xero had a profound impact on the accounting profession, LinkedIn has become a catalyst for change within the recruitment industry. Plus of course we are yet to see the impact that artificial intelligence will have on future recruitment processes.

However, as the old saying goes, 'all that glitters is not gold'.

Using internal resources to recruit

If you are planning on managing your recruiting internally, you usually have three options as to who you delegate this task to:

- the hiring manager (which may be you)

- your HR Manager

- your internal recruiter (if you have one).

Let's address a generic issue and then we'll look at each of the three options individually.

Active versus passive candidates

In recruitment land, we talk about 'active' candidates and 'passive' candidates. If you are going to manage your recruitment internally, you must first understand this distinction.

Active candidates are those people who are actively looking for a new role (makes sense, right?). They may be unemployed or simply keen for a change. These people are regularly checking job boards like Seek and LinkedIn and responding to advertisements. And while there are definitely some good active candidates from time to time, they are often not the 'cream of the crop'. Plus, when you advertise, you end up receiving lots and lots of applications from people who have no relevant experience (with a CEO role I am currently recruiting, 86 per cent of applicants have no relevant experience). Why on Earth these people apply for jobs they are clearly not suited for and will never be considered for is beyond me, however it happens all the time. Good people generally aren't actively looking for a new job. They are happily employed, have a good relationship with their boss, and are delivering good results. These people may move for a compelling reason, but they aren't proactively seeking a change. They are what we call *passive candidates*.

To attract passive candidates, you have to headhunt because they are not looking at or applying via advertisements. But it's very difficult to do the headhunting yourself because you can't maintain the confidentiality of who is hiring. Whether it is you personally or a member of your team reaching out to a passive candidate, of course they will immediately know who the employer is.

There are two problems with this.

Firstly, it's generally not a good look to be directly approaching your competitors' staff and trying to poach them. The breakdown of any kind of positive relationship, plus them reciprocating by directly approaching your staff, is almost certain. It also sends an immediate signal to your competitors about what is happening in your business. For example, when I was headhunted by other recruitment companies back when I was an employee, I would often meet with them just to gain competitive intelligence that I would immediately take back to my boss (see, I was both sneaky and loyal).

Secondly, passive candidates may have a preconceived idea of your company's culture, track record or other elements that would affect their perception of you as an Employer of Choice. Their next-door neighbour may have worked for your company 10 years ago, had – in their mind – a less-than-ideal experience, and this could dissuade your ideal passive candidate from wanting to apply for a role with you.

When you use a third-party recruiter, they can keep your company name completely confidential, both when advertising your role and when headhunting passive candidates. Good headhunters know how to appeal to a candidate's sense of curiosity, using the right bait to get them on the hook before telling them who the employer is. You simply can't do this yourself, and it can often mean the difference between an excellent shortlist and an underwhelming one.

The potential pitfalls of DIY

Let's assume however you do decide to manage the recruitment process yourself, rather than using an external agency. While recruitment is not rocket science (although by the end of this book I am sure you will agree it's not as simple as you thought), it is time consuming, especially if you want to do it well. So if you delegate recruitment to the line manager (which may be you), understand that it is definitely going to distract them from their normal operational duties. There can be a significant hidden (or not so hidden) cost to this. Can you actually afford to neglect all the other mission-critical tasks this line manager needs to do? Plus, recruitment is definitely a skill in its own right, and if the line manager is not skilled in hiring, or just doesn't enjoy doing it, you will probably end up with a suboptimal result.

Generally your HR Manager will be more skilled at recruitment, given it would fall under their mandate. And while most good HR Managers can manage the back end of a recruitment process well (interviews, reference checks, offer management and so on), they are generally far too busy with all their other tasks to do headhunting. As a result, you will generally be limited to only seeing active candidates who have applied to job advertisements, which as previously stated is not ideal.

Your final option is to employ and utilise an internal recruiter, most often someone who has an agency background however has decided to go in-house. And I'm now going to make one of my most contentious statements, which will no doubt anger some readers of this book.

Speaking generally, **internal recruitment is where most failed external recruiters end up if they stay in the profession.** There are definitely some exceptions, but they are few and far between. (Note that I am only referring to external recruiters who then go in-house, not to in-house recruiters who are developed internally.) The number of managers, including CEOs, who tell me they are completely underwhelmed by the work done by internal recruiters is mind-boggling. Complaints about both the quality and quantity of shortlisted candidates, massive delays in the hiring process, simple mistakes made which result in good candidates withdrawing pre- and post-offer, and the list goes on and on.

Think about it this way. A good external recruitment consultant can easily earn well over $200k per year. When I was employed as a recruitment consultant before starting my business, I and members of my team regularly earned more than the C-suite executives we were recruiting. Not only did we earn more, but we also generally worked a pretty typical Monday-to-Friday job, as compared to when I was a COO in the building services industry, where I was on call 24/7 and would work massive hours, and on weekends, regularly.

Good recruiters can earn as much if not more than successful real estate agents, without any evening or weekend work doing open homes. **Being a good recruitment consultant is a very well paid and great job.** So why would a good recruitment consultant go in-house, to earn a fraction of what they earn as a third-party recruiter? The short answer is that they wouldn't. As another old saying goes, 'if you pay peanuts, you get monkeys'.

This is not to say that internal recruiters are bad people or are intentionally performing poorly. In the main, they are under-trained and under-managed. Added to this, they may be looking after large volumes of vacancies, from receptionists to senior managers and everything in between. Plus line managers often treat them with a lack of respect, especially if the recruitment team is not run as its own cost centre and charging the line manager for their time, much like an external recruiter would.

Many internal recruiters want to do a great job, and if you invest in proper training and performance management they can be great additions to your business. Reading this book and implementing all the strategies I recommend will definitely assist you in getting far better outcomes from your internal recruitment team, so don't lose heart just yet.

How best to work with external recruiters

To reiterate, the purpose of this book is to educate you on how best to recruit for your business yourself. However, there may be times when it makes more sense to use an external recruitment firm. I would definitely recommend using an external firm if you are recruiting at the executive leadership or board level. Likewise, if you need to confidentially headhunt a replacement for someone you want to terminate, an external firm is the way to go.

Everything I am going to teach you about recruitment in this book applies equally when utilising an external firm. You will be outsourcing certain aspects of the process, and you should hold them to the same high standards you would expect if doing it yourself, if not higher. So rather than running through the complete recruitment process with an external recruiter lens here, I'll touch on the various differences and nuances of internal versus external as we work through each specific chapter.

However, there is one critical element of working with an external firm that I want to highlight here, which I believe is crucial to achieving the best possible result for filling your vacancy.

Contingent recruiters versus retained recruiters

Recruiters typically are engaged in one of two ways:

- The first are contingent recruiters, who are paid only on successful placement. They are usually not working on the role exclusively and can be competing against multiple other external recruiters, and even internal recruitment, to place their candidate and get paid. If they are unsuccessful, they have potentially invested a lot of time and resources for free. Seems pretty dumb to me, however most of the market works this way.

- The other type of recruiters work on an exclusive, retained basis only. The most common fee schedule is that they get paid a third of their fee on commencement of the assignment, the second third on delivery of the shortlist, and then the balance of their fee on successful placement.

There are other fee structures out there (we for instance offer three different levels of engagement), but the general rule is the recruiter is paid for the time and resources they commit to filling your role.

I only work on a retained basis. **I think contingent recruitment is a mug's game and any recruiter who offers to do this should have their head examined.** If you ask virtually any other professional services firm to complete a project for you (lawyer, architect, engineer, you name it), they will quite rightly expect to enter into a contractual agreement with you and be paid along the way for the work they do. Seems totally fair, doesn't it?

Occasionally law firms will ask me to recruit mission-critical roles for them. Often these roles have been vacant for months, if not years. Law firms rely on their lawyers to bill, to make their revenue targets and grow profit for the firm's partners. No lawyers means no income, and the partners have expensive golf club memberships and private school fees to pay. It's a tough life at the top.

Yet when I tell these lawyers they need to pay me a retainer, their common reaction is to baulk and tell me that they never pay retainers to recruitment companies. I actually love it when they do this, because it allows me to tell a very funny story (at least, I think it is hilarious, although they probably don't). This is how it goes:

Richard: 'Well, that's interesting because I'd actually like to engage you to do some work for me. I just murdered my next-door neighbour (too much Rick Astley blasting at all hours of the night) and I'd like you to defend me. What I want to do is engage five different law firms to represent me, and whoever gets me the lowest jail sentence I will pay. The rest of you work for free.

'So, would you like the work?'

Lawyer (going bright red in the face and clenching their fists as if ready for fisticuffs): 'Absolutely not. How dare you insult my profession and my tremendously important ego by even suggesting such poppycock!!!!!'

Richard (said with a straight face although smirking inside): 'Well then why on Earth would you expect me to?'

But, I hear you shout to the heavens, contingent recruitment is *awesome*. We can get lots of recruiters looking for us rather than just one, and we only pay when the role gets filled. That's an *awesome* arrangement.

Well, it can *seem* that way, but consider this for a second …

Contingent recruiters typically work on a very high volume of assignments at any one time, in most instances at least 20-plus roles. Why? Because they know that they will be lucky to be paid for one in five. They'll promise you the world and then go back to their office, throw a quick advertisement up on the internet, and do a cursory search on their database. They might call a couple of contacts and ask for some referrals.

Three days later, if they haven't found anyone suitable, they just move on. They stop returning your calls and replying to your emails. Or, even worse, they throw some irrelevant CVs at you, praying that, just like mud sticks to a wall, someone will stick and be hired. Often, they won't even interview the candidate first and you'll be left dumbfounded as to how they so misunderstood the brief and delivered you a big pile of rubbish.

In contrast, **a retained recruiter is committed to delivering you an excellent result** (at least they *should* be). They will only be working on a very small number of roles (in my business, typically less than four at any one time). They know they are working exclusively, and they are going to get paid, so they can commit their all to delighting you, leaving no stone unturned and delivering you an outstanding result.

Of course, if you are paying a retainer, you have every right to demand and expect exceptional service. Great, frequent, proactive communication and a commitment to delivering you a result.

If you are ever in a bar and you happen to be eavesdropping on two contingent recruiters chatting over a drink, the conversation will most likely go like this: 'Bloody employers, treating us like white-shoe used-car salespeople. Why don't they respect me and the work I do? Why won't they return my phone calls, agree to meet me, and shower me with affection and rich rewards for the amazing professional I am? Why is life so unfair?'

To which I would answer, 'Because you work for free, dimwit! What would you expect? You make promises you don't keep, and 90 per cent of you won't even be in the industry within two years. All because you don't charge what you are worth. Geez!'

Always retain your external recruiter exclusively to handle your assignments. You'll get a much better result, plus it's just good manners.

In this chapter, you have learned:

★ You can choose to hire a recruitment agency to fill your vacancies, or manage the process internally.

★ Organisations can save significant amounts of money by recruiting at least some of their roles themselves.

★ If a role requires headhunting due to confidentiality or for a rare skillset, using an external specialist headhunter is the right decision.

★ If working with external recruiters, *always* retain versus using contingency agencies.

Chapter 2

'Would you like to dance?': when should you start a recruitment process?

Many employers have a very reactive approach to recruitment. A couple of reasonable examples would be an unexpected resignation, or winning a major new project that requires quickly hiring some new staff to complete the work. In both of these scenarios, you can understand why the recruitment process is 'just in time' and needs a speedy outcome.

Yet I would say that in at least nine out of ten cases, when we are briefed on a role and I ask the employer ideally when they want the new employee to start, they say, 'yesterday'. Why is it that recruitment always seems to be urgent? Especially when you consider it could take a month to get to shortlist, another month to finalise an offer and do the deal, and then from one month up to in some instances six months for the new employee to fulfil their notice period with their current employer (especially if they are a senior executive)?

Consistently recruiting reactively is a poor business strategy. It typically ends up costing you more money, and is a huge distraction from other critical tasks you may be doing at the time. Sitting there in an anxious headspace desperately needing to fill a role is not great for your mental health either.

Always be recruiting

So when should you start? The short answer is that **you should be recruiting all the time**. You should be proactively allocating time every week to focus on your future human capital (workforce) requirements and undertaking specific tasks to ensure that you are never left in a desperate situation.

This could be as simple as committing to having at least one introductory coffee meeting with an up-and-comer in your industry each week. It might be attending an industry event or speaking at a conference once a month, and scouting out promising talent that you want to get to know. It might be talking to one recruiter in your industry a fortnight, getting the lay of the land and 'gossip' about who might be on the market and why.

Even in the reactive scenarios above, resignations rarely come completely out of the blue. Generally you'll have a sense of when people are disgruntled or getting itchy feet. Likewise, winning a major new project is not something that happens overnight. You should be planning for either of these, or other similar eventualities, and deciding on an appropriate course of action.

Another great saying: 'Those who fail to plan, plan to fail.' The last thing you need is to be caught out and needing to make an urgent hire. This will probably result in a suboptimal result, even potentially a poor hire that will see you having to replace the role again in a few months. And who's got time for that?

Ideally, you should allow yourself a minimum of three months to fill an executive role. Operational or lower-level roles can often be filled more quickly as generally these candidates have shorter resignation periods. However, if for example you are regularly recruiting forklift drivers, it would make sense to have some kind of recruitment campaign happening at all times, because these employees are equally likely to leave with minimal notice. If you have an internal recruiter, or are using external recruiters, this is called a 'watching brief'. Essentially you are instructing them to keep a constant eye on the market and to proactively bring suitable people to your attention. Once again, you will need to put an external recruiter on a monthly retainer if you want them to prioritise this for you.

But before you even start any kind of recruitment process, you need to ask yourself a pretty fundamental question: 'Why would someone leave their current employment to work for my firm, and me in particular? How can I position us as an Employer of Choice, so we are the logical first option for top-tier employees when they are ready to make a career change?' And guess what – this is not a job that you can simply outsource to HR, as you'll see in the next chapter.

In this chapter, you have learned:

★ The more proactive you are in your hiring practices, the more assured you will be of getting a good result.

★ Prioritise recruitment by factoring in certain activities like attending events, having coffee meetings or speaking to your preferred recruiters.

Chapter 3

Build it and they will come: positioning you and your business as an Employer of Choice

In this book I am going to regularly reference a guy named Lou Adler, an American recruitment expert who wrote a fantastic book called *Hire with Your Head* (John Wiley & Sons, 2007). Around the same time as his book was published, I had the wonderful opportunity to meet with and be trained by Lou when he visited Australia, something I will always be grateful for. In my opinion, his book is *the* recruitment bible and a must read for anyone who is serious about hiring excellence (maybe his book is the Old Testament and mine becomes the New Testament? What a sacrilegious thing to say).

The underlying principle of Lou's teaching is that the best predictor of future success is past success, so your goal should be to **hire people who have 'done it before, have done it well, and are motivated to do it again'**. I'm going to be drawing on Lou's wisdom often in this book.

To begin with, let's talk about Lou's 11-factor analysis that candidates use when comparing a potential new role to their current one, plus any other alternatives. I think it's a great tool and one I use in my recruitment and career coaching business regularly. In this instance I want to use this tool in the context of developing your Employer of Choice brand.

11 factors potential candidates will consider

If you are going to become an Employer of Choice you must be aware of Lou Adler's 11 factors a candidate will use, either consciously or subconsciously, when considering a role with your company. These are:

1. **Job match:** Can they actually do the job they are being employed to do?

2. **Job stretch:** Is there sufficient stretch in the role to keep them motivated and engaged?

3. **Job growth:** What are the future opportunities within the role or organisation?

4. **Hiring manager:** Who is going to be their boss, and do they like and respect them?

5. **The team:** Who will they be working with on a daily basis, and will they enjoy spending more of their time with them than with their family (assuming they work full time)?

6. **The executive leadership team:** What do they think of the CEO, the board and/or the company owners? What is their reputation in the market?

7. **The organisation's vision and values:** Do they believe in what the company stands for?

8. **Tools:** What tools will they be given to ensure they can do their job to the best of their ability?

9. **Remuneration and benefits:** Are they happy with the salary on offer and any other benefits (vehicle allowance, health insurance, annual leave provisions and so on)?

10. **Work/life flexibility:** Will they have the flexibility to manage family, sporting interests, study and other commitments? Of course this now includes working from home, telecommuting and so on in our post-Covid world.

11. **Risk:** Is there any perceived risk in taking this job? Relocation, redundancy, sale of the business and so on.

As you have probably just realised, being an Employer of Choice is not a 'one size fits all' solution. Every candidate is unique and as such their perception of each employer is unique, and much of this centres around each specific role rather than just a general perception of the organisation.

Later we will explore specifically how to use this 11-factor tool when engaging with prospective employees, managing an offer, and then retaining your top performers. In the meantime, I just want to focus on points four, six and seven – the hiring manager, the executive leadership team, and vision and values, as these are less role-specific.

Building your personal brand as a hiring manager of choice

Once again, I am initially going to draw on the expertise of someone way smarter than me, in this case Jim Lecinski from Google who wrote an excellent ebook *Winning the Zero Moment of Truth* (2011), which I highly recommend reading to learn more about this concept (it's an oldie but a goldie).

The Zero Moment of Truth is the first time a potential buyer (in this case a prospective employee, but it would also include prospective clients, suppliers, joint venture partners – everyone who deals with you in a professional context) seeks information about a particular product (you). The internet allows buyers to be able to seek information and opinions about things they want to buy before they make any attempt to actually engage in a sales process.

To use a consumer marketing example, let's say you want to buy a new car. When you go into the dealership, and see the car in the showroom, that is the 'First Moment of Truth', when you decide if you will buy it. Once you buy the car and take it home, the 'Second Moment of Truth' is when you own the car and decide how satisfied you are with the experience and product. As Jim Lecinski writes:

> Today's consumers know so much more before they reach the place of purchase. They find incredible detail online, from every possible source, about the brands and products that matter to them. They browse, dig, explore, dream and master, and then they're ready to buy with confidence. And what they learn, they share with others … those Zero Moments of Truth where first impressions happen and the path to purchase often begins.

How does ZMOT apply to your personal brand? In recruitment, the **Zero Moment of Truth is when someone looks at your LinkedIn profile** (plus potentially other readily available information about you on the internet). They are forming an opinion about you before they even have a conversation about you or with you.

Your LinkedIn profile

When a prospective employee looks at your LinkedIn profile, they are asking themselves, among other things:

- Is this person reputable?

- Can they mentor and coach me to achieve my highest potential?

- Can they solve the problems I am currently experiencing in my career?

So you need to make sure your LinkedIn profile can pre-emptively answer these questions as quickly and positively as possible, as they apply to your employees of choice.

There are many useful books about how to write an excellent LinkedIn profile, just as there are about how to write an excellent CV (one great book is *I'm On LinkedIn, Now What?* by Jason Alba). As such, I'm not going to focus much on that here, apart from making a few key points.

Firstly, **your LinkedIn profile should be as good as, if not better than, your current CV**. It should contain as much content as possible to best articulate your key achievements and skills. It should have a good-quality headshot of you in a professional setting (not running a marathon or playing with your dog). You should include plenty of detail on each of your historical roles, your professional qualifications and any professional memberships. Prospective employees want to know this stuff – they want to understand you as a person, what makes you tick and how your career has unfolded.

In short, **it should sell you as an exceptional boss and leader**, so that candidates are left with a high level of confidence that you are someone they would love to work for.

And yet most people's LinkedIn profiles are rubbish, with virtually no detail and nothing to catch the attention of future employees.

If you want to attract the highest quality of talent, you need to 'sell the sizzle, not the steak'.

Don't believe me? Have a look at the LinkedIn profiles of the CEOs of the ASX top 10 companies. All of them are absolutely terrible when viewed from a candidate attraction perspective. They have limited to no detail, often just a list of former job titles with nothing to indicate in any way why they or their organisation is an Employer of Choice. You would think that with the massive marketing budgets these companies have, someone would have taken the initiative to write a captivating and employee-attracting LinkedIn profile for their ultimate leader?

Some of them don't even *have* a LinkedIn profile, no doubt far too busy and important to deal with random people reaching out via LinkedIn to establish connections and build rapport. In today's world, it is inconceivable and, in my opinion, completely unprofessional to not have a LinkedIn profile. If you don't want to deal with spam and unsolicited connections, get your EA or someone else to deal with it. Seriously, this is not rocket surgery, folks!

What else can you do to build your profile as a hiring manager of choice? Here's just a few more examples:

- As mentioned previously, you can proactively seek opportunities to speak at conferences.

- You can appear as a guest on podcasts, or even host one yourself (I do and it's really fun).

- You could even write a book or two. I can't begin to tell you how much my first book, *Uncover the Hidden Job Market: How to find and win your next senior executive role*, did to lift my profile from being just another recruiter to an industry thought leader (did I mention I have sold or given away over 15,000 copies since it was published in 2015, and that a new edition came out in 2023?).

- A really easy thing you could implement immediately is to get your staff to write testimonials on your LinkedIn profile saying what a great boss you are. Imagine what 10, or 50, or even just a few of these would do to enhance your credibility as a leader. It's free and your staff will enjoy doing it for you (you might even choose to reciprocate).

There is almost an unlimited variety of things you can do to build your profile as a hiring manager of choice. Get creative, get proactive and have fun.

Building the executive team's (and board's) brand

When a prospective employee is researching your organisation, they are going to be interested in the reputation and experience of your board members, CEO and senior leadership team. Therefore it's important that they can access this information easily, and that when they find it this information enhances your attractiveness as an Employer of Choice.

So to begin with, **are the profiles of your board members and executive leaders on your company website?** Are they easy to find, rather than being hidden away in an annual report or on the investor relations page? Are they written in a way that would make prospective employees excited about joining your company? Do they 'sell the sizzle, and not just the steak'?[2]

Next, **does every member of your executive team and board have a LinkedIn profile**, and if not, why not? In my opinion, it should

---

2   As an interesting aside, I am amazed at how many companies, including significant ASX organisations, don't include their Head of Human Resources as part of the executive team on their websites. If your people are your greatest asset, surely this should be reflected in who you present as your executive team? What does this say about the level of respect within your business for the HR function? Definitely something to think about.

be mandatory that everyone not only has a profile, but that they have an *awesome* profile. Plus, there should be a consistent brand message across each person's profile. Organisations have brand style guides that stipulate the colours, fonts and tone of their marketing and other collateral, so why wouldn't you have the same thing for your leadership team's LinkedIn profiles? You won't really be able to get complete consistency across your board members' profiles, because they may sit on multiple boards, however the description of your specific business can be cut and pasted into each director's profile to ensure you are best promoting your organisation as an Employer of Choice.

Once again, remember that **LinkedIn (and your company website) are an integral part of your 'Zero Moment of Truth'**, so spending some time and money on getting the basics right is a great investment.

No doubt at least your CEO, plus potentially other members of your board and executive team, has been a guest on a podcast, spoken at a conference, appeared in an article or perhaps have even written and published material themselves. All of these things can be linked to your website plus your company's and individual LinkedIn profiles. If one of them has done something amazing, like completed a significant fitness challenge or raised a significant amount of money for a charity, promote it. Employees love this stuff.

Perhaps you could start a company podcast with episodes that are interviews with each member of the executive and board? Perhaps you could do video interviews that can be published on YouTube and your website? What other fun and creative things could you do?

Building your vision and values to position you as an Employer of Choice

I'm sure everyone who is reading this book has heard about the importance of vision and values. There are plenty of great books,

TED talks and other resources you can investigate if you're unfamiliar with what I am referring to.

If you're a bit older like me, you've probably sat through many workshops, executive retreats and strategy sessions over the years to determine or revise the vision and values for the organisation you were working for at the time. Great deliberation ensues, perhaps some heated debate, and eventual consensus. Everyone has a big group hug and a couple of drinks to celebrate.

I'd also guess that you saw the vision and values get printed on a poster, hung on the reception wall, and then promptly forgotten (are you getting the sense here that I'm a little bit cynical?).

As research for this section of the book, I had a look at many of the top listed and private companies' websites to see how they are promoting their vision, mission and values. Most make no reference to them at all. Then of course you get incredibly inspiring examples like:

- 'Our objective: to deliver a satisfactory return to our investors.'
  (Oh stop it, you're turning me on! Wow, where do I sign up?)

- 'Our core values: integrity, openness, accountability, entrepreneurial spirit.'
  (Could you be any more naff and contrived?)

Why can't your vision, mission and values be unique, inspiring and exciting? And clearly define you as an organisation and what you stand for? And that you can explain through the use of captivating stories, which can be front and centre on your website and excite people about wanting to work for you?

I used to work for a company that in my opinion had awesome values, which were explained through stories. One of their values was, 'Campsite Four'. This was a reference to the highest campsite on Mount Everest you reach prior to climbing to the summit. The explanation was that you needed to spend time at Campsite Four if you wanted to make that final push to the top of the mountain, but you didn't want to live there. It's a story about going the extra mile and doing whatever is required to get the job done, while ensuring that you don't burn out by spending too much time in such adverse conditions.

Now that's an exciting value with an interesting story.

This company had five clearly articulated values, and each one was unique and had a great story to accompany it. I would tell these stories to every new potential employee in their first interview. And do you know what? They loved it. These values were the foundation of our recruitment process and, coupled with the personal brands of the executive leadership team, made us a formidable employer.

Investing time and money to develop your own unique and inspiring vision and values is a critical element in attracting and retaining top talent. Great employees want to work for amazing companies that have inspiring values. 'Delivering a satisfactory return to our investors' just ain't going to cut it.

Once you've developed your own, share them loudly and proudly on your website, LinkedIn profiles and other marketing collateral. Create great stories and maybe you can record some videos or podcasts to share these stories with your employees, clients and other key stakeholders.

I'm going to be talking more about values as they pertain to leadership later in the book, however for now let's move on.

In this chapter, you have learned:

★ Prospective employees are assessing both your profile and your company's to decide if you are their Employer of Choice.

★ Use your company website and LinkedIn profile to clearly articulate why your company is a great place to work.

★ Use tools like podcasts, videos, speaking at conferences and testimonials to further build your employer brand.

★ Have a vision, mission and values that are exciting and help you stand out from the crowd.

Chapter 4

Begin with the end in mind: briefing a role for success

You now understand when you should outsource your recruiting and when to DIY the process. It's time to go to the market and find an exceptionally talented person to fill your vacancy. So **the first thing you need to do is actually work out what you want.**

Formulating a good brief (essentially an explanation for who you want to hire and why) for a role is not difficult, however it's amazing how few companies do it well. If you don't have a clear and comprehensive brief, how can you expect the people to whom you have delegated the recruitment process to, to deliver a good result? I regularly speak to internal HR and recruitment team members who don't have more than a rudimentary awareness of what the hiring manager is looking for, gleaned from a position description (an overview of the role and responsibilities) and perhaps a quick chat. Likewise, I frequently receive feedback from senior candidates that they have been approached about a position by third-party recruitment consultants who can't speak authoritatively about the role and who simply don't understand the position they are recruiting for.

As I have mentioned previously, the best predictor of future success is past success. You want to find someone who has done it well before, and is motivated to do it again. A good brief begins by outlining clear, quantified, performance-based outcomes for the position being recruited. It's ideal to break these down into the first three months, the following three months (months four to six), and then 12 months. Essentially, what you should be asking yourself is what will my new employee need to achieve for me to be delighted with their appointment?

A brief must be unique to your company and circumstances

Position descriptions, while useful, are typically made up of a bunch of what I call 'motherhood statements'. They provide a broad description of the role and accountabilities, but not much actual detail. They are generally pretty generic.

For example, a position description for a Sales Manager would probably include deliverables like:

- Create and execute a strategic sales plan that expands our customer base and extends the company's global reach.

- Meet with potential clients and develop long-lasting relationships that address their needs.

- Recruit sales representatives, set objectives, train and coach them, and monitor their performance.

While these points are definitely accurate, they apply to any Sales Manager position in any organisation. **Your vacancy is specific not only to your business but also to that particular point in time**, and as such each brief is going to be unique.

As an example, let's say three different companies are recruiting a new Sales Manager. They all work in a similar industry, and all use a fairly generic position description for the role. However, all three may have very different requirements in terms of successful key deliverables. Let's pose a question to each of these companies: 'For you to be delighted with your new Sales Manager, what would they have needed to deliver in the first three months?' Here's three potential responses:

- *Company one:* 'Our previous Sales Manager resigned a few months ago and this has left the business in a fairly poor state. The sales team has not been performing well and retention is poor. We believe the people are good, and they want to do well, however they have been lacking good leadership and vision for some time. An early priority is to assess the sales team members for competency and commitment; then to build a shared vision for the team and get them re-engaged. If within 90 days the Sales Manager can report back to me that their team are now excited about the future and committed to achieving their goals and budgets, that would be a great result.'

- *Company two:* 'The business has been going through some challenges. While we were the market leader, new technology has allowed our competitors to really reduce their costs and we are being consistently beaten on price. What we need the Sales Manager to do is quickly identify every opportunity we have to trim costs, while still ensuring we are delivering excellent service to our existing clients. A great result within 90 days would be to know clearly how we are going to reduce our operating costs by at least 25 per cent within 12 months.'

- *Company three:* 'The business has been going great. The team are performing really well, and our clients love us. We see a great opportunity here to really leverage our existing business and increase our revenue by moving into some new markets, either geographically or by adding some additional products and services. What we would like the Sales Manager to do in the first 90 days is meet with all our major clients and then formulate a strategy for improving revenue and market share. Revenue growth of at least 10 per cent in 12 months would be an excellent result.'

You can see that even though the organisations operate in the same industry, and the role of the Sales Manager as described by the position description is very similar, the key deliverables are vastly different. This will make a huge difference to who you hire, which we will talk about in the interviewing section of this book.

A brief must involve key stakeholders

It is also really important to have all key stakeholders participate in preparing the brief, because there may be differences of opinion as to what deliverables are actually required. It's essential that any disagreements get resolved, and that there is consensus and clarity prior to commencing the recruitment process. Otherwise you may face frustrations, and potentially derail or delay the hiring process further down the track.

A few years ago I was retained to recruit the new CEO of a prestigious membership club. This club has a voluntary executive committee (similar to a board) with a new president being appointed every 12 months. In this instance, the selection committee for the recruitment of the new CEO was made up of the immediate past president, the current president, and the vice president (who would become the new president the following year).

When I met with these three people to take the brief, I asked them collectively what success would look like in the role. What were the key deliverables they wanted their new CEO to achieve? While in broad strokes they concurred on most of the deliverables they required, they each had a unique viewpoint.

The immediate past president had been a member for many years. He was a gentleman who had been very successful in business and was a refined and conservative man. His response was, 'I want someone who understands and appreciates the values and traditions of the club, and who treats our members and guests with the highest of respect'. He wanted someone who would continue to deliver the traditional club environment and offerings to members, which he and his friends had enjoyed for a long time.

The current president was their first ever female president, and a highly respected and successful board chair and director. Her professional background was as a partner with a Big Four accounting firm. Her response was, 'I want someone with strong financial acumen, who can provide the committee with much greater visibility on the financial performance of the club, so we can make informed decisions about how best to manage and improve the club from a financial perspective'.

The incoming president was a former managing partner of a highly successful law firm. His response was, 'I want someone who can be a catalyst for change. We need to modernise elements of the club to continue to appeal to a changing demographic, otherwise our ability to attract and retain younger members may be negatively impacted'. He wanted someone who knew how to run successful and innovative food and beverage venues that young professionals would want to join.

As you can see, if I had been briefed by only one of these people, instead of all three, it would have significantly skewed the type of candidates presented in the shortlist. By having all three of the key decision makers participate in the brief, I was able to deliver candidates who had attributes that met all three criteria.

So a great brief, documented as a performance profile, will clearly articulate the key deliverables required over the first 12 months and potentially beyond. The brief should also include all the necessary information around location, salary and other benefits, size of team (if applicable) and any other relevant information for the role. (I have included three examples of performance profiles at the end of this chapter.)

A brief must specify required experience and attributes

Another critical consideration is the past experience and attributes of the preferred candidate. I typically ask this question: 'If I could wave a magic wand and the perfect candidate walked through the door, describe them to me. Where have they worked, what are their qualifications, and what are you looking for from a cultural fit perspective?'

Recently we recruited a new CEO for a privately owned mining equipment hire company. When I met with the Managing Director and one of their key investors, I asked them to describe the perfect candidate. They said it was mandatory that the person had already been a CEO and had direct experience in leading an entire business, with full P&L responsibilities, and who had reported to a board.

Not long after we had commenced our search, the MD said his accountant had recommended someone for the role. When I looked at this person's LinkedIn profile, they were a Chief Financial Officer with a retail company. In other words, they did not meet the brief at all! Let's just say that after reviewing the brief and the key deliverables required with the MD, he agreed that perhaps this particular candidate was not really the person he was looking for.

On the other side of the coin, a couple of years ago I was asked to recruit a Chief Operating Officer for a trade services company (they provide electricians, plumbers and other trades for predominantly residential work). The owners said that the COO must be a qualified tradesperson, to understand the business and have credibility with the team. Without going into a long story, I convinced them to interview a former lawyer from a business-to-consumer services background. He had extremely good experience in marketing these types of businesses, and they ended up hiring him. They realised that the trade qualification was not actually critical after interviewing a number of tradespeople who lacked the track record in achieving the results they desired.

What I am illustrating here is that just because you have defined at the beginning of a recruitment process what the ideal candidate looks like, this doesn't have to be set in stone. Your priorities and opinions may change over time, especially after you interview some candidates. Often meeting people that you subsequently decide you don't want helps you to decide what you *do* want.

If you have delegated the shortlisting of candidates to a member of your team or a third-party recruiter, it's important you respect them as a trusted advisor. In both examples above I was able to challenge the employer and together we achieved a great result.

Why would this person choose to work for you?

The final element to a great brief is to ask the question, why would this person choose to work for you? What are you offering that is attractive enough for them to leave their current job and boss, both of which they may still like, to join your team? This is called the 'employee value proposition'. Remember, we are definitely targeting passive candidates here, not just those applying to your advertisement. However, even active applicants have options and want to be convinced that you are the right choice.

This is where your positioning as an Employer of Choice becomes critical, as well as being able to articulate role-specific attractors.

When I initially ask the question, 'Why would someone leave their job to come to work for you', most employers say something pretty mundane. 'Because we are really good', 'Because we care about our people', 'Because it's a great career move', and the like. All may be true but they aren't really going to do much to convince a top-tier candidate.

Take the time to identify some compelling reasons why someone would join you, and of course make sure you deliver on these. If you make statements that aren't true and you have no intention of delivering, you are going to end up with a disgruntled new employee and be back in the market looking for someone else pretty soon.

Performance profiles

Let's look at some examples of real performance profiles for roles I have recruited. A couple of points to note. Firstly, the performance profiles shown on pages 56 to 65 would normally include a lot of detail about the client organisation, however I have removed this for confidentiality. Secondly, the examples I have provided are for very senior executive roles (CFO, CEO and COO), however the principles remain the same for more junior roles, and you should be completing a performance profile for every role you are recruiting.

In this chapter, you have learned:

★ A great brief requires you to become very clear about what the key deliverables of the role are – what does success look like over the first three, six and twelve months?

★ Have all key stakeholders contribute to determining these key deliverables to make sure everyone is on the same page.

★ Also clearly identify the preferred professional background and experience, qualifications and any other prerequisite skills and attributes you are looking for.

★ Recognise that your preferences may change as you consider and potentially meet with candidates.

★ Ensure you develop a compelling employee value proposition – why would this person want to give up their current job to come and work for you?

Performance profile example one (to be used in conjunction with the position description)

Company:	**Mining Services Company**
Position title:	**Chief Financial Officer**
Location:	**Brisbane, QLD**
Reports to whom:	**CEO**
Remuneration:	**$300k including superannuation; plus, STI circa $100k (carpark included)**
Direct reports:	**3 Functional Areas (IT/Commercial/Finance) – total team circa 17**

Background

This role is to replace the incumbent interim CFO, who has been in place for approximately 4 months since the exit of the permanent CFO. The CFO is responsible for three work streams, being:

- IT – team is split between Brisbane and regional Queensland. Currently a predominantly outsourced model, there is a strategy now in place to move towards predominantly inhouse. Team performance is good.

- Commercial – Warehousing, Procurement, Contract Management, Payroll, etc. Team performance is good.

- Finance – Accounting, Treasury. The debt arrangements are complex with 22 banks across the world, and equity debt from preferred stakeholders. Team performance is good.

Historically, the teams within the CFO's mandate have been operating largely in silos, with limited involvement in the broader business. While progress has been made in breaking these silos down, the new CFO will need to have the leadership and relationship/stakeholder management skills to continue to integrate their teams into the overall business, demonstrating value through the provision of great services to the rest of the business.

The CFO is part of the Executive Leadership Team and participates in board meetings. Their soft skills around leadership and stakeholder management are critical, given the level of external relationships (banks, insurance, the board) and internal relationships necessary to do the job well.

$450 m in revenue

$3.5 to $4 b in assets

Circa 100 FTE

$3.5 b senior debt facility across global lenders

Key deliverables

Within 3 months

- Get their 'feet under the table'.

- Foster great relationships between the three teams to ensure good engagement and outcomes for the rest of the business. Build relationships based on trust, integrity and quality service delivery. Model the right behaviours to their teams.

- Continue to drive the insourcing project currently underway with the IT team.

- Complete the annual business planning cycle for board approval.

6–12 months

- Complete EOFY requirements.

- Ensure compliance to new changes in accounting standards.

- Execute the Annual Insurance Programme.

- Investigate and make recommendations as to how to grow the capacity of the company's operations. Enter into new contractual, commercial arrangements with key contractors etc.

- Look for continuous improvement opportunities within the team.

Ideal candidate

- CFO or 'step up' experienced in infrastructure or related business with complex debt funding arrangements. Does not have to come out of the coal/mining industry. Also, IT management experience is less of a priority than someone who shows excellent people leadership and stakeholder engagement skills.

- Excellent financial and commercial experience, especially around debt facilities, cashflow forecasts, and managing banking relationships.

- Will need to travel to regional Queensland 1 to 2 days per fortnight; Sydney (to meet with banks) 1 to 2 days every couple of months; and an international trip (Singapore/London) for 7 to 10 days each year around September.

Employee value proposition

- For a less experienced CFO, opportunity to grow and gain additional skills, dealing with external and internal stakeholders, a broad range of accountability, and an organisation that works essentially like a listed organisation.

- For a more experienced CFO, some big goals including the need to reduce debt; and to grow the business through greater utilisation of the terminal, so some big projects here to keep them interested and occupied.

Performance profile example two (to be used in conjunction with the position description)

Company: **Global Construction Services Company**

Position title: **CEO**

Location: **Brisbane**

Reports to whom: **US-based COO – global parent company**

Remuneration: **Circa $300,000 + bonus program (last year delivered additional US $200k linked to P&L results), 50% of bonus is delivered immediately and the remainder delivered in 2 years' time.**

Direct reports: **3 General Managers, CFO, Head of Operations, Head of Technology and Head of HR**

Background

The CEO position has become available as the incumbent CEO is retiring from the role and they will continue in a consulting role to the business.

Key deliverables

Within 3 months

- Win the respect of the Senior Leadership Team – 3 General Managers (one looking after Industrial Vertical including minerals and resources, one looking after the Bridge Vertical and one looking after the Commercial Vertical). Also reporting to the CEO, is the CFO, Head of Operations, Head of Technology and Head of HR who are all based in Brisbane. Head of Operations looks after back office operations in Manilla, Bangkok and Chennai (India). The team is currently performing at 9 out of 10.

- Review the calendar year budget – they run a calendar year rather than financial year budget. Currently on target which is $65 m, however some concern is in place surrounding the impact of the coronavirus.

- Get arms around Chennai and Phoenix. Chennai is the jewel in the crown delivering the highest quality work with the lowest production cost.

- Head of Operations wants to reduce workload from June, so a succession plan needs to be devised.

- General Managers are responsible for Business Development and Account Management. The CEO has predominately been internally focused through the merger; however, an expectation now is that the CEO will become more outwardly focused on strategic business development and key account management in the future.

Within 6 months

- Look at year end to make sure they meet budget. Plan 2021 budget and be on track to achieve goal for 2022 which is $100 m revenue.

- Be spending approximately 40% of time with external client focus engaging with CEOs of various clients internationally – examples include Jacobs and Worley Parsons. This will require about 1 week per month of travelling (1 week in 3 in first couple of years).

- Maintain a strong focus on retaining the key people in the leadership team.

Within 12 months

- In 2021, Chennai will grow from 350 to 450+ permanent employees. Look at a subcontracting strategy, for outsourcing work to allow for growth and scalability without having to employ their own direct staff.

- Future planning and looking at 'what if' scenarios for examples if different market segments go into recession and planning out scenarios to deal with that.

Ideal candidate

- Comes from a 'servant leader' mindset, not an alpha leader.

- Qualified engineer preferably civil or structural however mechanical is fine.

- Worked for substantial engineering consulting firms e.g. Jacobs, Worley Parsons, Arup in a General Manager or higher level with full P&L responsibility.

- Broader project focus and managed a wide range of people in different locations and ethnicity.

- Worked client side will be highly regarded however not mandatory.

- Someone who combines process and construction engineering experience with direct experience working on construction projects, client side, to understand the inefficiencies and effect of pulling different 'levers' on project outcomes.

- Professional humility, honesty and integrity, lead by example, strong work ethic.

Employee value proposition

- Create a legacy as the business has a great reputation and is financially successful.

- Fair amount of autonomy with limited oversight and involvement from the US parent.

- We work in a borderless world, so an opportunity to set up offices in Europe or other areas as appropriate.

Performance profile example three (to be used in conjunction with the position description)

Company: Residential trade services

Position title: Chief Operating Officer

Location: Brisbane Head Office

Reports to whom: Managing Director

Remuneration: Open to paying what is required (initial thoughts circa $225k base package)

Direct reports: 7 (total staff circa 180)

Background

The growth of the business, plus the MD's desire to now focus on some special projects for the company, has resulted in the role of COO being newly created. There is a genuine expectation that the role will transition to that of CEO once the successful candidate has fully integrated into the business and demonstrated success in the COO role.

Key deliverables

Within 3 months

- Get their 'feet under the table'. Meet and develop a rapport with all internal stakeholders including the leadership team and teams of tradespeople. It's important to note that this will be the team's first new boss in 10 years, so ensuring that there is consistency in management style from MD to COO, with a strong emphasis on maintaining the existing culture, is paramount.

- Become fully conversant with the existing management tools and daily KPI measurement systems (there are currently 100 daily KPIs measured).

- Become fully conversant with the unique sales systems utilised by the trades teams, from initial enquiry to on-site value-add approach, that has driven the success of the business, as evidenced by over 75% of new clients coming from referrals.

- Have successfully recruited positions required in finance team.

- Understand and agreed delegations of approval table.

- Determined and agreed communications methodology with MD.

- Start to identify ways to improve the existing operations, based on experience, and make recommendations to the MD and leadership team.

Within 6 months

- Have successfully taken over all ad hoc tasks from MD, including HR/IR issues, customer complaints, insurances and legal issues.

- Have gotten into a good daily/weekly rhythm with Mark in relation to meetings, reporting and management of priorities.

- Continued evaluation of all areas of the business and sharing of ideas for improvement with MD and management team.

- Worked closely with the Training and Marketing Managers regarding their 12-month rolling plans.

- Taken full accountability and responsibility for the balance of 2019/2020 budget including making recommendations for any alterations to forecasts.

- Having now operated under the existing management tools and daily KPI measurement systems for a few months, make recommendations for improvements.

- Have become fully conversant with the requirement to increase or decrease SEO/SEM spend on a daily basis based on current levels of bookings (generally working three days ahead).

- Have become fully conversant with the existing individual employment agreements and understand why these suit the business far better than EBAs.

- Have finalised the current special project to flowchart and put on SharePoint the whole of business activities.

Within 12 months

- Have taken fully COO accountability and be on pathway to CEO.

- Be contributing to the determination of future growth strategies for the business, which may include investigating geographic expansion, new business offerings, acquisitions and/or franchising. Note there is a preference for organic growth rather than seeking external funding.

Ideal candidate

- Must come a senior Operations Management background in the services industry, ideally B2C.

- May have a Trades background, however if so, must demonstrate the ability to remain 'off the tools'.

- May have tertiary business qualifications although not essential for consideration.

- Must have excellent financial literacy, coupled with full P&L responsibility, and understand the key drivers.

- Must have managed similar or larger teams of employees.

Employee value proposition

- A fantastic opportunity to join a market-leading company with a great culture.

- Clear pathway to CEO.

- Greenfield opportunity to make their mark, in supporting the MD around future strategy for the organisation.

- Excellent remuneration package including incentives.

- Potential for equity in the future.

- Potential relocation assistance for candidates from East Coast of Australia.

Chapter 5

Now comes the fun part: sourcing the best talent

You have now completed the brief and clearly defined the key deliverables you are looking for your new employee to achieve, what the ideal candidate looks like (background, qualifications, cultural fit and so on), and your employee value proposition. Now it's time to go to the market and start sourcing candidates for the role.

There are many ways to source great candidates. In this chapter we'll look at the four key options:

- referrals
- advertising
- LinkedIn
- headhunting.

If the recruitment process is confidential (either someone is currently in the role you want to terminate, or you don't want the market and in particular your competitors to know what you are doing), this will obviously have a bearing on your sourcing strategy. We will address this as we go.

Referrals

The first, cheapest and fastest option to source candidates is to leverage both your networks and those of your team, your peers, the senior executive team and board. Simply asking these key stakeholders who they know who might be suitable and available is a great way to uncover top-tier candidates. After all, if the candidate is recommended by someone already invested in you successfully filling the role, you can assume any referrals are definitely worth considering.

Some companies offer financial incentives to staff to refer people they know for current vacancies. In some instances these incentives can be thousands of dollars. From my regular conversations with CEOs and business owners, these incentive schemes have mixed success. My personal opinion is that your employees should be loyal and enthusiastic advocates for you as an employer, so why do they need a financial incentive? Does providing a financial incentive actually produce the wrong behaviours, where your employee makes a recommendation and introduction from a financial motivation, rather than what would actually be best for you or the candidate? Something to think about.

Advertising

The next thing you can do is advertise the role. Back in the olden days when I started my career with a recruitment company, it was all about putting an advertisement in the newspaper. We were brainwashed into selling press ads, firstly for the revenue, but mainly because it was a great way to promote the name of our recruitment company, piggybacking on the advertising spend of the employer client. Did you ever notice how the recruitment company's logo seems to take up at least one-third of the total advertisement size? Cheeky monkeys, those recruiters!

Of course, print advertising has gone the way of the dinosaurs and now it's all about internet job boards. In Australia, seek.com.au continues to dominate, although many companies are now choosing to advertise on LinkedIn as well as, or instead of, Seek. My experience to date has been that Seek generally provides a better result than advertising on LinkedIn, however it is more expensive and, depending on how popular that particular job function is, your ad can slip down the list pretty quickly (unless you pay a premium, as each new ad that goes up will be above yours in the search results). LinkedIn however is integral to candidate identification and attraction, and we will explore this a bit later on.

Remember, you are looking to attract the best candidates, not just those actively looking for a new job. Passive candidates, as described earlier, are *not* currently looking for a job, so it's highly likely they will never see your ad in the first place. As such, advertising roles on the internet can generate some quality candidates, however it's very hit and miss. You do not want to rely only on advertisement responses. Sadly, most companies do, and in addition the quality of their ads is generally average at best.

If you are going to advertise, make sure you do it right. Take a few minutes now to jump on Seek and have a look at a few job ads, both to better understand the points I am about to make, plus you might just find yourself a fantastic new job (I'm joking, okay?). I for instance have just gone online and looked up the first 10 General Manager roles listed. Here's a few general comments to begin with:

- **Most job advertisements are simply a regurgitation of the position description**, with very limited additional detail about the key deliverables of the role. As such, they don't really give candidates a good sense of what they are actually being employed to do.

- **Most job advertisements do nothing to sell the employer's value proposition as an Employer of Choice.** Maybe a paragraph is grabbed from the company website, but it's typically bland, boring and uninspiring.

- **A lot of job advertisements by third-party recruiters are so sparse, you can't even work out what industry the role is in.** This is a common ploy by contingent recruiters, who don't want their competitors identifying the client so they can present their own candidates and steal the recruitment fee.

- This one is the one that drives me (and all good candidates) *crazy* – when employers are advertising their own roles, **in almost all instances there is nobody's name and phone number on the advertisement for a candidate to call and ask questions.** This is also becoming increasingly the case with third-party recruiters as well.

I gave a presentation a few years ago at the Australian Human Resources Industry Association conference on how to attract and retain top talent. Speaking to an audience of about 300 HR and internal recruitment staff, I asked them why they didn't put their names and contact numbers on job advertisements. One brave woman put up her hand and said, 'I know we should Richard, but I just don't want to talk to candidates'. And if you think she is the exception versus the rule, have a look at Seek. You might also want to look at the job ads that your internal recruitment team are putting out there.

Imagine this scenario: a really great, top-tier candidate just happens to be having a look through Seek. They are not really pro-actively looking for a new job, as their life is pretty good, they are being well remunerated, and they like their boss. However, if something excellent came along, they wouldn't say no.

They see your role on Seek and think it could be interesting to learn more about. They can't really determine from the ad what the role actually entails (it's just a copy-and-paste position description), they can't determine the size of the team, who the role reports to, the remuneration, and plenty of other information they would want to know before they decide to make an application, especially if it's with a competitor.

They think to themselves, 'I know, I'll ring the internal HR/recruitment contact and ask them a few questions'. But lo and behold, there is no-one's name or phone number for them to call. So what do they do? They don't apply, and you miss out on potentially hiring an *awesome* new employee.

Or think about this scenario (which I hear about almost daily from excellent senior candidates): 'Richard, I applied for this job eight weeks ago with (pick your company of choice, because almost all employers are guilty of this). I have not even had an acknowledgement of my application, let alone an update as to the status of my application. I have no idea if I am even being considered for the role, and there is no-one's name or phone number that I can call to ask. This company is obviously a terrible employer and someone I would never want to work for.' And they go on to tell that story to anyone who wants to listen, trashing the company's brand as an Employer of Choice.

Imagine how much damage is being done to that company's reputation. And before you say 'that would never happen at my company', you might want to think again. When you have an internal recruitment team managing your recruitment process, I would *strongly* recommend you do some investigation about this.

Think about it this way: if you were a candidate, would you like to be treated like this? If your answer is 'no' (which I truly hope it is), you should be ensuring that your applicants are not being treated like a commodity by your company.

Recently I wrote this post on LinkedIn:

RANTS FROM AN EXECUTIVE RECRUITER – A MESSAGE TO MY INTERNAL RECRUITMENT COLLEAGUES OUT THERE

You have taken the time and expense to write a job ad and put it on Seek or LinkedIn. The idea is you want to attract high quality candidates, right? Yet high-quality candidates often want high-quality information before they choose to apply for a role, especially if it's with a competitor or they are not actively looking.

High-quality candidates want to pick up the phone and call a REAL person to ask REAL questions about a role, before deciding whether to apply.

But guess what? I would say that 95% of the time, internal recruiters (i.e. those who work directly for the employer) don't put their name or phone number on the ad. And when I question them as to why, they say that it's because they don't want candidates to ring them!

Can you imagine how many high-quality candidates you are missing out on by not putting your name and phone number on the ad? Would it be too much for me to say that you are actually doing a disservice to your employer by intentionally limiting your applicant pool? Let alone a disservice to your candidates, who expect and deserve to be treated professionally and with courtesy?

Think about what you would want if you were applying for a job. I hope that you would want to be able to call and speak to the recruiter managing the vacancy. Right?

IF YOU DON'T WANT CANDIDATES TO CALL YOU, MAYBE IT'S TIME TO FIND A NEW CAREER?

#why is this so hard to understand?

#am I the only one feeling this?'

My post was read by over 13,000 people and received 50 comments, almost all from senior executive candidates. Here's a couple of examples:

> Excellent point Richard Triggs – I totally agree. I've also had the experience of ringing & emailing the listed contact – with no response & on a few other occasions I've rung the company directly to ask who is the best person to speak to and/or address the application to and have been told to just address it to HR (& that no one is available to talk to about the position). When this happens, I don't end up applying as I value my time and experience.

> Totally agree Richard Triggs, I have steered clear of jobs ads that don't disclose any contact information and identify who they are.

There was one comment from an internal recruiter who had worked for two of the largest ASX-listed companies in Australia. She subsequently deleted her comment, but it read something like this:

> It's all well and good for you Richard to make these disparaging comments about internal recruiters, however you need to understand that I am managing between 30 and 40 vacancies at any one time, plus juggling internal meetings, training and a host of other responsibilities. I simply have no capacity to take calls from job applicants.

Interestingly, the companies she had been working for consistently have great challenges in filling their vacancies and both have been in the news within the last 12 months for major problems largely exacerbated by poor hires.

If you are too busy to handle candidate enquiries, put someone else's name (your EA or a more junior member of the HR team) and their number on the ad and give them enough information to be able to answer most general enquiries. It's pretty simple and will dramatically increase both the quality and quantity of applicants, plus treat respectfully those people who have applied. This is exactly what I do in my own business, and it works fantastically.

My views on this are pretty black and white – if the person empowered to manage your recruitment process refuses to put their name and phone number on the advertisement, *fire them!*

At the end of this chapter, I've included a few examples of advertisements I have written for the same roles I offered as examples of performance profiles in the previous chapter.

LinkedIn

LinkedIn has been an absolute godsend to the recruitment industry, although third-party recruiters were extremely averse to it at first. I remember attending a recruitment association (RCSA) conference not long after the LinkedIn Recruiter subscription license came out around 2015. I had been a strong advocate of LinkedIn from the very beginning, and I had (and still have) a very friendly and positive relationship with LinkedIn senior leadership in Australia. Sitting with them at dinner each night, I was stunned and quite disgusted with the vitriolic abuse these LinkedIn employees faced from my peers in the recruitment industry, who felt that LinkedIn was literally killing their businesses.

Fast forward to today and recruiters, both in-house and third-party, heavily rely on LinkedIn to do their jobs, and for very good reason. LinkedIn, and in particular the Recruiter subscription, has given recruiters unprecedented visibility and access to employees, all over the world, virtually instantaneously. A few keyword searches and we can build out a list of prospective candidates with a fraction of the effort required in the past.

Pre-LinkedIn, searching for passive candidates was hard. Big global recruitment companies like the SHREK brands (Spencer Stuart, Hedrick and Struggles, Russell Reynolds, Egon Zender and Korn Ferry – see, their initials spell SHREK – cool huh?) needed teams of researchers to map markets to identify talent. They believed they needed their big blue-chip brand names to entice these passive candidates into a conversation. This is why they would say they needed offices in every major capital city in the world; recruitment consultants (called Client Partners and the like) who had come from senior executive roles in industry; 12 weeks to deliver a shortlist; and as a result they needed to charge upwards of 25 per cent to 40 per cent of total remuneration package as their fees.

Quite frankly, this might have been true back in the day but it's complete BS now. My team can map a market in a matter of hours (globally in a couple of days); candidates couldn't care less if they are talking to me from Arete Executive or from some hotshot blue-chip firm (they just care about the opportunity); and we guarantee to deliver a shortlist in 20 working days. If you are continuing to pay exorbitant fees to the SHREK brands, you may want to ask yourself why.

Anyway, jumping off my soapbox, LinkedIn is awesome. It's not the be all and end all, as not everyone has a LinkedIn profile or keeps it up to date. There are definitely other ways to identify passive candidates, like looking at companies' websites, looking at delegates at conferences, and other means to work out 'who's who in the zoo'.

LinkedIn Recruiter licenses

Likewise, you don't need to purchase a LinkedIn Recruiter license to undertake searches for candidates, however it does make a big difference. These licenses aren't cheap; depending on what kind of package and how many licenses you have they are around $1000 per license per month. A Recruiter license allows you to undertake very comprehensive searches using a variety of keywords, to save identified suitable candidates into a project folder within LinkedIn, and then send these candidates InMails (the LinkedIn version of emails). It's very fast, and depending on how competent you or your recruitment team are, it can be very thorough.

I could write an entire book on how to use LinkedIn Recruiter, but there are already great resources out there, including LinkedIn themselves, who can teach you how to use it. Suffice it to say if you are recruiting regularly, it is definitely worth the investment. If you have an in-house recruitment team, I'd almost guarantee you already have at least one subscription and they are using it on a daily basis.

However, the way most in-house recruiters utilise LinkedIn has its limitations, which you need to be aware of. Firstly, let's assume that your internal recruiter has used LinkedIn to build a list of potential candidates. The next thing they will do is send InMails to these people asking if they are interested in your vacancy. As soon as they send an InMail, the approached candidate is going to immediately know who you are as the prospective employer because they can see which company the person sending them the message works for. So there is no ability to remain anonymous, and for the reasons I have mentioned earlier this can be an issue.

Secondly, I don't know about you, but I receive hundreds of emails a week. Those that are critically important will get dealt with immediately, while others may sit in my inbox for weeks before being actioned. When you add on top of this all the unsolicited InMails I receive (a lot being spam), it's completely overwhelming. So I, like so many busy professionals, have turned off the function where LinkedIn redirects InMails to my normal email inbox. In other words, I only see my InMails when I actually go into LinkedIn and check my messages, which could be weeks after someone sends me a message.

Why is this important? Because your in-house recruiter may very well have sent an InMail promoting your vacancy to an identified candidate, but if they don't see it they won't respond. Likewise, if they are not actively seeking a new role and are busy, even if they see the message there is a high likelihood they won't bother to respond. So InMails (and emails) in and of themselves are not much better than advertisements, in that if your preferred candidate is not actively looking for a new job, they won't even see it, or even if they do they probably won't apply.

Let's say as the hiring manager, you delegate candidate sourcing to your HR or internal recruitment team. A couple of weeks later when you enquire as to how things are going and when can you expect to see a shortlist, the person recruiting the role tells you that ad response has been average and that even though they sent a bunch of InMails to prospective candidates on LinkedIn, the response rate was low. So with a sad face they give you a few underwhelming CVs to consider and tell you this was the pick of the bunch. But, 'Hey dude, it's a war for talent'.

This is why for difficult-to-fill or confidential roles, it's absolutely mandatory that you *headhunt*, which is where LinkedIn really steps up to the plate.

Headhunting

I love headhunting. There's nothing better than calling someone in their workplace and engaging them in a fantastic conversation that ends up with them taking a new role with my client. It's a great win/win for all parties – except perhaps for their former employer.

While some recruiters will skirt around the topic of headhunting, not really wanting to admit to it as if headhunting is some kind of evil and malicious practice, **I wear the title of 'headhunter' with pride**. Earlier in my career, when I was working for another recruitment company, I used to run an internal group called 'Headhunting is not a dirty word!'

I happily tell the market that there are 'some companies I *invite to lunch* (my clients), and some companies that are *on the menu* (those I headhunt from)'. And before you express your discontent that I would engage in such terrible behaviour, understand that if you treat your staff well and they love their work, they won't want to be headhunted and will politely decline my offer. Nobody is being coerced to do something against their will.

Also, ethically I will never headhunt from my clients. I know other recruiters do this, including some who even headhunt candidates they have placed in their client's businesses. For me, this is totally unacceptable, totally unethical, and I don't condone this behaviour at all.

If you are utilising in-house recruiters, and if you want the highest quality and quantity of candidates for your vacancy, they must headhunt. Relying on ads and InMail responses is simply not sufficient.

Yet there are two issues with utilising in-house recruiters to headhunt:

- The first is exactly as I have previously stated, in that they can't maintain confidentiality. If they call someone to pitch an opportunity they will reveal their employer. This is not necessarily an insurmountable issue as you may not be concerned about confidentiality. But a third-party recruiter like me uses confidentiality as bait to draw in my target, because they are curious to know more (it's exactly the same with InMails, by the way).

- The second issue is that headhunting takes a lot of time. While we may be able to draw up the list of targets quickly, it may take multiple phone calls before you even connect with the prospective candidate to have a conversation. In some cases you can almost feel like a stalker. If your in-house recruiter is busy, with lots of competing priorities, they probably won't have the time to do it properly and comprehensively.

Also, **most recruiters (especially in-house recruiters) hate to headhunt**. It can be awkward, and push them outside their comfort zone. A common response when I ask someone to headhunt is, 'but what if they are too busy or not interested in talking to me?' Noting that most recruiters are younger and/or don't have a lot of professional experience, they may feel too shy or inhibited to call a more senior executive. Or they may just be too lazy, which is probably most often the case.

But I think making a headhunting call is great fun. What's better than calling someone and giving their ego a stroke by telling them you potentially have a great job for them? Most people are happy to receive the call, happy to hear what I have to say and appreciate my interest in them, even if they aren't interested in the role I have to offer. It's extremely rare that someone has become angry with me and told me to get lost. Even if they did, so what? There's plenty more fish in the sea.

How to headhunt properly

Of course, if you are going to headhunt, you want to do it properly. What I generally do is find the target person's work email address. This is fairly easy to do using free websites like Email Hunter (https://hunter.io), which will help you identify the company's email protocol (for example, firstname.surname@companywebsite.com.au). If that doesn't work, you can always ring the company's switchboard and ask for the person's email address. Pretty simple stuff.

I then send an email along the lines of:

Hi Nicole,

I've been engaged to recruit a new Logistics Manager for an FMCG company in Sydney. I would really appreciate five minutes of your time to discuss the opportunity and ask your advice about where I may best identify suitable candidates. You may even have someone that you can refer. Please let me know the best number to call you on. If I don't hear from you in a couple of days, then I'll follow you up with a call on your landline.

Regards, Richard

Note in my email I have not said I want to headhunt them, because their EA or someone else from their company may have access to their emails. Instead, I am asking for their advice. Again, this is a nice ego stroke and I tend to get a good response. Plus, if they are interested in the role themselves, they will generally reply very quickly.

Alternatively, I may want to be more proactive and call them directly, especially if I have been able to find their mobile phone number (from a referral, or on their LinkedIn profile or company website, for example). In this instance, my opening line tends to be:

Hi Nicole, we haven't spoken before. I'm an executive search specialist and I've been engaged to recruit a new Logistics Manager for an FMCG company. **If I could demonstrate this job is better than your current one, would you be interested in speaking to me?**

What an absolutely awesome line that is – it almost always gets a positive result. Who is going to say no to that? Once they say yes, I ask if it's a convenient time to talk now or whether we should schedule a call for when they are less busy? After all, I have called them out of the blue and they are probably in the middle of doing something else.

When we do speak in more detail, I can then engage them in a conversation to explore what they would need in order to consider another opportunity and whether in fact my vacancy fits the bill. If it doesn't, that's totally fine and I'll use the opportunity to ask for referrals.

Headhunting is fun, it almost always gets a better result in relation to the quality and quantity of candidates, and recruiters who enjoy and are good at headhunting are worth their weight in gold. You will need to develop this skill in your in-house team if you want to be able to consistently attract the best candidates.

Hiring for true diversity rather than just ticking a box

Over my 20-plus years as an executive recruiter, it has been interesting to watch the evolution of the debate around diversity in the workplace, especially at a senior executive level. What was once regarded as 'nice to have' has now become in many instances mandatory. On multiple occasions we have been engaged by ASX100 companies specifically to headhunt women for key appointments to meet a gender diversity target.

Now diversity extends far beyond just gender to include sexual orientation, ethnicity, age, people with disabilities and increasingly people from an Indigenous background (especially at board level). I'm certainly a big advocate for diversity and highly encourage our clients to step beyond their traditional avatar of what makes a good employee.

It's also essential that there is a commonsense approach to ensuring that even when hiring for diversity, the appointed candidate is equally well credentialled based on merit. These people definitely exist. The challenge becomes how to find and attract these people to your organisation.

Here's a real-world example:

A few years ago I was at a gender diversity debate dinner, one of only a handful of men in a room surrounded by at least 150 women. It would be fair to say there was a lot of heated commentary about the 'patriarchy', the 'glass ceiling for women' and similar statements. So I decided to do a bit of an investigation.

In the previous month, we had recruited four C-suite roles (CEO, CFO, COO and the like), three of which were for not for profits. In every instance, the client had specifically said that they would love to employ a woman. Across the four roles, we had 800 unique applicants to our advertisements. What percentage of these do you think were women? Seven per cent! Fortunately, we are headhunters, so we are not reliant on ad response to fill our vacancies.

If women truly want these opportunities yet aren't applying, what's going on? This is definitely a generalisation, but often if a female candidate reads an advertisement that calls for ten criteria and she believes she only has seven or eight, she often won't feel it's worth applying as she is underqualified. On the other hand, if a man reads the same advertisement and believes he only has three, he'll think he's absolutely the best candidate for the job! (Once again, yes, I know I'm generalising, however it is a common scenario.)

What's the answer?

If you legitimately want to hire for diversity, you need to accept that you are very unlikely to get the right quality and quantity of candidates from advertising alone (whether you're seeking gender diversity or otherwise). You need to headhunt these people because they are generally in higher demand, not actively looking, and may be less likely to apply (as mentioned above).

Hiring for diversity is an excellent thing. Hiring exceptionally talented people who have proven key achievements and transferable skills is also a great thing. Don't fall into the trap of hiring people purely to achieve a diversity target. Employ the best person, who also happens to bring diversity to your team. Hiring policies that include both attributes, versus one or the other, is where the gold lies. Do this consistently and you will have an amazing business.

In this chapter, you have learned:

★ There are three main ways to source candidates: referrals, job advertisements and headhunting.

★ Referrals are a great way to generate candidates quickly and cheaply. Make sure you consider and speak to all the key stakeholders who may know the right people to approach.

★ When advertising, make your ads interesting, compelling and comprehensive.

★ ALWAYS ALWAYS ALWAYS put a person's name and phone number on the ad to handle enquiries and maximise the quality and quantity of your candidate pool.

★ LinkedIn is a fantastic tool for headhunting, however just sending InMails isn't enough. Your recruiter needs to pick up the phone and call passive candidates.

★ If the role is confidential or hard to fill, consider engaging a third-party specialist headhunter.

Advertisement example one:

Chief Financial Officer – Major Infrastructure company – Brisbane

- Lead Finance, Commercial and IT teams
- Significant experience in complex debt funding arrangements required
- Circa $300k plus incentives salary package

You are a highly skilled CFO with excellent leadership and stakeholder management skills. You have had significant experience in managing the broad range of CFO responsibilities, plus managing debt funding arrangements and banking relationships. You enjoy having a strategic orientation to your role, supporting your organisation in looking for opportunities for operational and financial performance improvement. You ideally come from a large-scale infrastructure background (resources, transport and logistics, construction etc.), although this is not mandatory for consideration.

Here is your opportunity to join a significant Queensland infrastructure company, reporting to the CEO and based in the Brisbane CBD head office. This is a complex business with multi billions of dollars in assets, circa $500 million in revenue, and multi billions of dollars in senior debt across global institutional lenders. You will be leading a large team across finance, commercial and IT functions. This is a business that is running well, with a very positive story in the marketplace.

To be successful in the role, you must be a proven leader, able to develop and maintain an excellent culture of service, trust and accountability. There are many external stakeholders with a broad range of interests, so you must be able to manage these relationships and competing priorities to ensure the overall success of the organisation. You must have the ability to do regular, short-term travel (one to two days) interstate, and an annual international trip (seven to ten days).

On offer is an excellent salary package plus lucrative incentive programme, a highly successful and respected senior leadership team, and the chance to really make your mark. This is a great opportunity for you to grow your career due to the broad mandate of the role and develop the skills necessary to ensure a career path to the highest level.

Please submit your CV for consideration, or call Richard Triggs to make an enquiry.

Advertisement example two:

Chief Executive Officer – Global Engineering Company – Brisbane head office

- Global market leader in their field

- Circa 1000 FTE, $50m plus revenue

- Excellent salary package plus performance bonuses

You are a qualified Engineer (civil, structural, mechanical) who has managed large geographically dispersed teams and has held full P&L responsibility in substantial organisations. You may already be a CEO, or this could be your 'step-up' opportunity. Ideally your experience includes working for large Consulting firms, and working on construction projects, client side, to understand the efficiencies and effect of pulling different 'levers' on project outcomes. Your leadership style is one of supporting your teams to achieve their full potential and you are a strong supporter of diversity in the workplace.

Here is your opportunity to join a truly global firm, with their head-office based in Brisbane. They are regarded as the market leader in their space, with a strong history of delivering world's best-class, iconic projects. You will be managing teams based internationally across the globe (circa 1000 FTE and $50m plus revenue), with your direct reports industry specialists sitting across specific vertical markets. The business is in excellent shape, highly profitable and with a clear vision of the future.

With a high-growth agenda and the launching of new, non-core services to greatly enhance their ability to be a trusted advisor to their clients, you will be focused on identifying further opportunities for international expansion. You will also enjoy taking a lead role in key account management at CEO level with existing and prospective clients.

To attract the highest calibre of candidates, on offer is an excellent salary package plus substantive performance bonus. To be considered for the role, you must be able to travel regularly internationally (anticipated circa one week in three initially). Relocation assistance is available for candidates not currently in Brisbane.

Please submit your CV for consideration, or call Richard Triggs to make an enquiry.

Advertisement example three:

Chief Operating Officer – B2C Services Company – $30m turnover

- Brisbane-based role managing a team circa 180 staff
- Newly created role reporting to MD
- Clear succession plan to CEO

You are a highly experienced senior Operations Manager, with significant career achievements in leading service-based businesses, ideally within Business to Consumer (B2C) environments. You understand the critical importance of delivering exceptional customer service within sales-led cultures. You have excellent financial skills, knowing the key drivers that make service businesses successful. You have led large teams of people and have a passion for organisational culture.

Here is your opportunity to join a market leader within their industry. The business has grown to the point that the Managing Director has created this COO role, to take accountability and responsibility for managing the general operations (including sales), as well as playing a part in determining the future strategy of the company. The business is in great shape financially and has some very exciting new opportunities to explore moving forward.

Reporting directly to the Managing Director, it is intended that the role will transition to becoming CEO. You will be leading a team of approximately 180 employees being predominantly 'in the field' staff, plus head-office personnel including finance, sales and marketing. The organisation has a reputation for an exceptional culture, centred around best-practice training for all employees. Employee satisfaction and retention as a result are excellent, as is overall profitability.

On offer is a very generous remuneration package including incentives, a clear pathway to becoming CEO, and the opportunity to really make your mark as the business grows into new markets and service offerings.

Please submit your CV for consideration, or call Richard Triggs to make an enquiry.

Chapter 6

'It's lovely to meet you': engaging candidates into your process

At this point your candidate sourcing process starts to pay dividends and you are receiving applications. The two main priorities now are ensuring that these candidates have a positive experience, and separating out the high-potential candidates from those you are not interested in pursuing further.

Every candidate should receive a rapid acknowledgement of their application. It may be an automated system (for example, our CRM database immediately sends an email on receipt of an application) or it may just be a cut-and-paste email sent by whoever is managing the recruitment process for you. The email gives peace of mind to the candidate that their application has been received, plus it can also convey information about the recruitment process. It can help to position you further as an Employer of Choice.

Here's an example:

Dear XXXX,

Thank you so much for taking the time to submit an application for the role of XXXXXX. I commit to responding to your application within seven days, either by email or phone call.

Regards
(name and contact details of internal recruiter or
person responsible for recruiting the role)

(See what pushback you get from your recruitment team members about putting their name and contact details on these emails. If they are actually committed to ensuring your business is regarded as an Employer of Choice and candidates feel valued, they will be delighted to do so. If not …?)

The next thing to do is begin to separate the stronger candidates you wish to bring forward for interview. Removing those applicants who are completely unsuitable for the role is a pretty easy process. I'm sure everyone reading this book who has done at least some recruiting will be as incredulous as I am as to why some people apply for jobs they are totally unqualified for. We call these applicants 'tyre kickers'.

Narrowing the field

When ranking applicants, we use a traffic light system in my business. These applicants are coded RED for unsuitable and are sent a TNT (Thanks but No Thanks) email almost immediately.

Dear XXXX,

Thanks again for submitting an application for the role of XXXXXX. Unfortunately in this instance there were more suitably qualified candidates and as such we will not be proceeding with your application. I wish you all the best with your job search.

Regards

(name and contact details of internal recruiter or

person responsible for recruiting the role)

It can be tricker, however, to get from a longlist of potential candidates that look promising on paper to a shortlist of candidates you actually want to interview. Let's say you have a couple of GREEN candidates (these people look very suitable based on their CVs) and then a bunch more ORANGE candidates (not sure – needs further investigation).

My recommendation is that you have someone in your team (the internal recruiter if you have one) call these applicants and conduct an initial telephone screen. Within 10 minutes they will be able to glean enough information to help you determine who should be on your final shortlist. In my business, I have one of my team ring every GREEN and ORANGE candidate and ask five questions:

1. 'Why are you looking for a new job?'

2. 'Give me a sense of your current responsibilities – size of team, budget, geography (whatever is relevant for the role)?'

3. 'Were you to be successful in getting the role, what is your notice period/timeframe to commence?'

4. 'What salary package are you ideally looking for?'

5. For the fifth question, the person doing the screening should be given two of the key deliverables from the performance profile

to ask about. For example, let's say you are recruiting a CFO and one of the key deliverables is the implementation of a new ERP system. The question would be, 'Can you give me a short example of a time in your recent career when you have successfully implemented a new ERP system?'

Another key deliverable might be to build a much better relationship between the finance team and the operations team, so they would ask for an example of this.

Remember, according to Lou Adler, you are looking for people who have 'done it before, done it well, and are motivated to do it again'. Asking these questions will give you a quick insight into who is worth bringing forward for a full interview.[3]

This is also an opportunity to answer any questions from the candidate and finish the call clarifying next steps. For example, the candidate could be told that all initial calls will be completed by the close of business next Friday and that they will be contacted the following week with an update on whether they will be interviewed or not. This buys you time, as the candidate won't be hassling you for updates, plus it gives them peace of mind.

Always remember the market is moving very quickly, and great candidates have plenty of options, so you need to move fast. My recommendation is that candidates should be screened within five days of their application, *at the latest*. If you snooze, you lose. Jump on these candidates, especially the GREEN ones, immediately to avoid losing them to a competitor.

When it comes to asking a candidate what remuneration (salary package) they are looking for, as a general rule they will always talk

---

3   I am not saying you dismiss any candidate who hasn't done before *exactly* what you need them to do. This might be a step-up role for them, in which case you are looking for evidence that they have the right foundational skills and experience, and they are growing in their career. Alternatively, this might be a lateral move for them from another industry or role family, in which case you are looking for key achievements that demonstrate they have *transferrable* skills.

it up (especially if they have been headhunted). Candidates will inflate what they want because, hey, why not? Your recruiter needs to take control here and bring the candidate back to reality.

Let's say I am recruiting an Operations Manager and the proposed salary is $200k to $250k. I'm screening a candidate (or talking to a headhunted candidate) and I ask them what the salary would need to be for them to move. They tell me '$300k'.

> *Richard:* 'Thanks Fred, I appreciate that. Let's say that this role ticks every box – great company, great team, great future, it's literally your ideal job, but it only pays early $200s. Are you saying that you would not want to be considered?'

> *Fred:* 'Ooh … ahh … mmm … No, I would definitely still like to be considered.'

> *Richard:* 'Excellent.'

Of course, if the person is adamant that they want $300k and you can only offer $200k, there is no point in wasting everyone's time. You are better off using the opportunity to ask for any referrals of people who perhaps are earlier in their career (that is, want less money) and then let the candidate you are speaking with move on.

Other candidates won't want to disclose their salary expectations, which is fine too. In that case, just be honest about the range on offer. If they choose to withdraw from the process yet you think they are *awesome*, you can always reconsider the package and go back to them. Candidates you have headhunted need to be managed differently. After all, you reached out to them, not the other way around. They won't appreciate it if after being headhunted, they get a call from a junior staff member and are being asked to prove they are worthy of consideration. So keep these candidates aside from this process. It may well be that, post the screening calls, you believe there are better applicants than those you have headhunted, and if that's so then you can deal with this accordingly.

Once all the screening has been completed, your recruiter (if you did not make the calls yourself) can provide you with a report and talk you through each of the applicants and their recommendations as to who you should shortlist for interview. They may have screened up to 20 candidates and from their feedback you can bring it down to the shortlist (potentially three to six candidates) that you want to conduct a formal interview with. This saves you a huge amount of time and ensures you are only interviewing candidates who have been pre-qualified as meeting the brief and who are positively motivated about your opportunity.

Those people that have received a telephone screening call, or who were headhunted and are no longer desired for the shortlist, *must* receive a call (rather than an email) to give them the news that their application is no longer being considered. These people invested time in the process, and they will want feedback as to why they are no longer being considered. It's the right thing to do and will protect your Employer of Choice brand. If your recruitment team are not currently doing this, ask why.

In this chapter, you have learned:

★ In the current market, move fast to ensure you don't lose candidates to your competitors.

★ At every touchpoint, treat your candidates as you would wish to be treated – acknowledge their emails, return their phone calls and deal with them in a timely manner.

★ Having a team member perform a high-quality telephone screen with preferred candidates will save tremendous time in your recruitment process.

★ Headhunted candidates will need to be managed differently from your general applicants.

Chapter 7

Oprah, eat your heart out: interviewing excellence

Now things are getting really exciting. You have an awesome shortlist of candidates to interview, and the finish line is in sight. Your vacancy is going to be filled, all your pain is going to go away, and you've already booked that long-overdue holiday. You can feel the sand between your toes and taste the piña colada on your lips. That sweet, sweet taste of success! (Do you ever have these thoughts during a recruitment process or is it just me? Perhaps I need therapy?)

First things first: what is going to be your interview process? Are you just going to do one round of interviews, or will the candidates have multiple interviews? Who is going to participate in the interviews? Are you going to use an interview panel? What kind of questions are you going to ask? Will psychometric testing be part of the process, and if so, at what point? There's lots to consider.

How many interviews?

Let's start with how many interviews. Largely this depends on how senior the role is and how many stakeholders are involved in the recruitment process. For example, if you are recruiting a more junior role, one interview is probably sufficient. If you are recruiting a mid-level manager, you would probably want to complete one interview as their immediate line manager and then perhaps a second with them plus another key stakeholder.

If you are recruiting a CEO, you will want to do multiple interviews as this is such a critical role, plus CEO candidates will require multiple conversations to meet their own due diligence requirements. Coupled with this would be the signing of non-disclosure agreements so that the candidate can see financials, business plans and other documents they may require.

Who is going to conduct the interviews?

Secondly, who is going to conduct the interviews and, more importantly, have they been trained in how to interview well? Just because your Operations Manager is great at leading her team, it does not mean she is great at interviewing candidates. In fact, I would say it's highly likely that she is not. Likewise, don't assume that just because someone has an HR degree, or they have some recruitment experience, that they are great at interviewing. **Being a great interviewer is a skill, and leaders need to invest time in building these skills.**

I would recommend that the initial interview is done by the line manager (which may be you), potentially with their HR counterpart present as well. It's always good to have a second set of eyes and ears. If you are recruiting a CEO or you're the type of organisation that likes using interview panels, there may be three or four people present.

Any more than this can be intimidating for the candidate, and I don't recommend it.

I don't recommend that HR does the first interview alone. They have already done the screening call, so having them subsequently doing a full interview on their own seems superfluous. However, if HR are available to participate in your interview with the candidate, that is a worthwhile thing to do. If nothing else, it's a great opportunity for them to learn more about what you are looking for in a candidate, for future sourcing.

If there are multiple people in the interview, decide what role each person will play, and what questions they will ask. You don't want to look disorganised, plus you want to be efficient and make best use of the time.

Running the interview

Again, I want to refer to Lou Adler's seminal masterpiece, *Hire with Your Head*, a 300-page deep dive into interviewing excellence. If recruiting is something you do regularly and/or you want to develop interviewing mastery, I strongly recommend you read his book. For now, I'm going to share some of his ideas, adding some of my own perspective based on my 20 years' experience.

People love to do what they are good at, and they love to talk about it with pride. If you can get someone to talk about what they love to do, and it matches what you want them to do, then voilà – you've potentially found an excellent new employee for your vacancy.

How does this work in practice? This is how I typically run my interviews and it will demonstrate what I'm talking about.

After meeting the candidate and building rapport, I'll explain the structure of the interview, what I'm hoping to achieve, and let them know they will have plenty of time for questions. I will typically say something like, 'Sally, we have a lot to achieve in this hour so if at any point I seem to be rushing you along, I apologise in advance. I just want to make sure that we make the best use of this time. Is that okay?'

I then say, 'Please give me a five-minute maximum overview of your career history to date. I'm not looking at this point for any detail or deep dives on any particular roles, just give me a walkthrough of your career.'

I set a five-minute limit because otherwise they could spend 20 minutes talking about their first few jobs and I just don't have time. If they start to get bogged down, I can remind them of our agreement about me rushing them along and they typically are fine with me doing so.

Once that has been completed, I then use Lou Adler's killer question, which forms the basis of his performance-based hiring methodology:

> Sally, what I would like you to do now is to tell me about a recent key achievement in your career, say in the last five years, something you are really proud of, that you would hang your hat on and say, 'this is why I am excellent at my job'. It could be a new initiative, a special project, whatever first comes to mind.

And then Sally, who loves what she does and loves to talk about it, starts telling me a story. She delightedly tells me about one of her key achievements and I'm fascinated to listen. As she tells me this fantastic story, I can ask her some probing questions, like:

- What were some of the challenges you overcame?

- What results did you achieve?

- How long did it take?

- What skills did you need to apply?

- Who was in your team?

- What did you most enjoy doing?

- What did you least enjoy doing?

- In hindsight, what would you have done differently?

(For a full list of potential questions, refer to Lou's book.)

What I am looking for is evidence that what they love to do, and are good at, matches what the employer has determined the key deliverables to be for the role we are trying to fill. Let's go back to my earlier example of recruiting a new Sales Manager. One company needed someone to rebuild the team and culture, one company needed someone to reduce costs by 25 per cent, and the third company wanted someone to launch new products into new markets.

Let's say that when Sally starts to talk about her key achievement, she tells a story about how she successfully launched a new product into a new market, and the fantastic results she achieved. This is awesome if that's what the employer wants, however if they want someone who can reduce costs, she is probably not the right person.

I'll now investigate Sally with a similar question based around an actual key deliverable the employer wants. So I would say, 'As you know from reading the performance profile document I sent you, one of the key deliverables my client wants is to identify ways to reduce their costs of goods sold by 25 per cent. Can you tell me about a specific key achievement of yours that relates to that?'

Sally can then go into this story and it's going to be immediately fairly obvious whether she has in fact done this before. If she hasn't, a call needs to be made as to whether she is worthy of further consideration.

Can you see what a great way to interview this is? It's a much more relaxed and positive experience than bombarding a candidate with a bunch of dumb and irrelevant questions, like:

- 'What are your five greatest strengths?'

- 'What type of leader are you?'

- 'If you had to describe yourself as an animal, what kind would you be and why?'

Crap interviewers ask crap questions. What I love about performance-based interviews is that they cut straight to the chase – what does this person love to do, and do they love to do what I want them to do? Simple, clear, easy to do in a panel situation, and easy to assess and compare with other candidates.

Why is this person looking for a new job?

One of the other things I want to understand at the interview is, why is Sally looking for a new job? I know she has already been asked this during the screening call, however I want to dive deeper. I want to gather information about how she perceives her current role and employer. Lou's 11-factor analysis mentioned previously is the tool I use for this, with a different emphasis. A reminder:

1. **Job match:** Can they actually do the job they are being employed to do?

2. **Job stretch:** Is there sufficient stretch in the role to keep them motivated and engaged?

3. **Job growth:** What are the future opportunities within the role or organisation?

4. **Hiring manager:** Who is going to be their boss, and do they like and respect them?

5. **The team:** Who will they be working with on a daily basis, and will they enjoy spending more of their time with them than with their family (assuming they work full time)?

6. **The executive leadership team:** What do they think of the CEO, the board and/or the company owners? What is their reputation in the market?

7. **The organisation's vision and values:** Do they believe in what the company stands for?

8. **Tools:** What tools will they be given to ensure they can do their job to the best of their ability?

9. **Remuneration and benefits:** Are they happy with the salary on offer and any other benefits (vehicle allowance, health insurance, annual leave provisions and so on)?

10. **Work/life flexibility:** Will they have the flexibility to manage family, sporting interests, study and other commitments? Of course this now includes working from home, telecommuting and so on in our post-Covid world.

11. **Risk:** Is there any perceived risk in taking this job? Relocation, redundancy, sale of the business and so on.

I probably won't explicitly ask her questions around each of the 11 points, however I will subtly guide the conversation to get as much information as I can. Why do I want this? To make sure that I can best present the employer and role as ideal for her, plus to pre-emptively deal with any counteroffers (more about this later).

Let's assume Sally is looking for a new job because she feels overqualified for her current role, there's no opportunity for career progression, and she is worried the company may be heading for tough times. Great to capture for future reference.

Timing the interview

Make sure you leave enough time to allow the candidate to ask any questions. Don't fill the entire hour (or whatever you allocate) with your questions of the candidate. Even worse, hiring managers often start an interview by telling a big, long, convoluted story about the business, themselves, the reason the position became available and other information, meaning that the actual interview isn't even an interview at all. They don't end up asking any real questions of the candidates because they have run out of time. This happens all the time – don't do this!

After the interview

Post interview, it's important to gather your thoughts about that candidate. If you wait until you have completed all the interviews, you may forget some relevant information. You may also succumb to what is known as the 'halo effect', where one particular candidate stands out and as a result you can tend to disregard the others rather than assessing everyone properly.

Lou Adler has another great tool for this, called his '10-Factor Analysis' (there's a copy at the end of this chapter). It is a table you can use to evaluate each candidate against 10 different criteria:

1. Technical skills

2. Motivated to do the work

3. Team skills

4. Problem solving

5. Achieved similar results

6. Planning and executing

7. Environment and cultural fit

8. Trend of growth (of career)

9. Character and values

10. Potential and summary.

For each criterion, the candidate is ranked from one to five. Basically, those who are ranked as one or two are unqualified and incapable of doing the job and should be excluded from any further consideration. At the other end of the spectrum, those ranked as five are probably too good or too big for the role and it will be difficult to retain them, so they should be excluded too.

What you are looking for are candidates who rank predominately as three or four for each criterion. These people can do the job well and they will probably hang around.

If you have multiple people attending the interviews, this tool is great for avoiding groupthink. Whenever I participate in a panel, I ask all the interviewers to intentionally not share any of their thoughts between the interviews. At the end of each interview, each panel member fills out their 10-factor sheet for that candidate. At the conclusion of all interviews, a roundtable discussion of the various merits of each candidate is done, using the completed forms to allow for comparison. It is a fantastic tool for identifying differences of opinion, resolving these and getting to consensus.

Subsequent interviews

If you choose to conduct further interviews with the preferred candidate or candidates, these will generally be more informal and less structured. Ideally the original interviewer will participate in these and brief the other attendees, so the candidate doesn't feel they are being forced to repeat themselves. It might be that the line manager does the first round of interviews, further tightens the shortlist to one or two final candidates, and then they meet again and include the line manager's boss (which could be the CEO/MD). Top-tier candidates know they have lots of options. They need to be sold on the opportunity. They need to be managed through the process with precision and loving kindness.

These people are going to massively improve your world, so ensure they are delighted.

Too often recruitment processes drag out. Candidates aren't communicated with promptly. There is too long between interviews. The employer doesn't provide any feedback. They get sent dumb, automated emails from CRMs that aren't relevant. The list goes on and on. These people are your greatest asset and need to be treated accordingly.

Here's a great story for you. A few years ago, I was coaching the CEO of a substantial mining company through their job search (let's call him John, although that's not his real name). A client partner (glorified recruitment consultant) from one of the SHREK brands (the five blue-chip global search brands) contacted this CEO, John, asking him to be an applicant for a CEO vacancy with another substantial Australian mining firm.

John told the SHREK consultant that he was happy in his job, extremely busy, plus he already knew from gossip in the market that the mining company looking for a new CEO had an internal candidate they were going to give the job to, and that the external recruitment process was them purely going through the motions to appease shareholders.

The SHREK consultant told John this was definitely not the case, his client had specifically said they definitely wanted to interview John, and that John had a high chance of getting the role. So John said he would travel to Melbourne to attend the interview, on the basis that he would go a day earlier to meet with the SHREK consultant and prepare together for the interview.

This was a role with a base salary of almost $2 million per annum, and the SHREK firm would been getting a recruitment fee of at least $500k, so it was a big deal.

John flew down to Melbourne the day before the interview to meet with the SHREK consultant. He arrived at their office to find out that the SHREK consultant was not even there. It turned out they had completely forgotten and were having the day off to play golf. As you can imagine, John was not impressed.

John goes the following day to be interviewed by the board for the new CEO role. He leaves the interview feeling positive and genuinely excited about the opportunity. With no further correspondence from the SHREK consultant for over a month, he then finds out that the internal candidate did in fact get the job.

Can you imagine how furious John was? He had taken time out of his extremely busy life, been stood up by the SHREK consultant, and then finds out that his original reservation about participating in the process was completely vindicated.

Do you think John will ever use that firm as a client in the future? Do you think he speaks kindly about the mining company he was interviewed by? This is a real example of what happens all the time, with candidates feeling completely let down by the process and how they have been treated. Please don't do this.

In this chapter, you have learned:

★ Plan your interview process – how many interviews are held, who is going to be present, what format you will take and so on.

★ Don't assume someone who is excellent at their job is necessarily excellent at interviewing. Being a good interviewer takes skill, so upskill your hiring managers accordingly.

★ People love to talk about what they are good at, so Lou Adler's one-question interviewing technique is a fantastic way to get the information you need for your selection process.

★ Once again, treat your candidates with the utmost respect to protect your Employer of Choice brand.

Factor	Level 1 Unqualified	Level 2 Less qualified	Level 3 Fully qualified	Level 4 Highly qualified	Level 5 Super star
1. Technical skills	Incompetent. Below minimum standards	Can do the work, but needs added support	Can perform all required work very well	Does more, better, faster	Leader in field. Sets the bar
2. Motivated to do the work	Lazy, passive, doesn't want to do the work	Will do the work if urged or pushed	Self-motivated to do this type of work	Takes initiative to do more, faster and better	Totally commited to get it done
3. Team skills in similar groups	Uncooperative, bad attitude, hides problems	Will cooperate if asked. Needs urging	Fully cooperates, handles conflict	Takes initiative to help others. Motivates	Inspires, coaches. Asked to lead
4. Problem solving, thinking	Misunderstood issues, no solutions	Barely understood issues. Superficial. Weak solutions	Understood all issues and had good solutions	Quickly understood issues with great solutions	Understood all issues. Optimises results
5. Achieved similar results	Experience and accomplishments are a total mismatch	Some comparable accomplishments. Needs training	Handled similar projects with very good results	Environment and projects match with strong results	Scope, culture match with exceptional results
6. Planning and executing	Unorganised. Weak planner. Very reactive	Reactive, misses deadlines	Good organiser, meets deadlines, prioritises	Anticipates problems, beats deadlines	Great execution. Optimises results
7. Environment and cultural fit	Complete mismatch on culture and environment	Reasonable match on culture and environment	Good match on pace, resources, culture	Very successful in this type of culture	Thrives in this type of environment, culture
8. Trend of growth	No personal or business growth noted	Flat trend. Capable needs pushing	Growth trend is consistent and positive	Strong upward growth trend. Wants more	Great upward trend. Needs big opportunity
9. Character and values	Questionable character, job doesn't fit values	Job somewhat fits values and needs	Strong fit on values, motivating needs	Job clearly meets values, motivating needs	Great character. A role model
10. Potential and summary	The job is over person's head	Barely handle job, unlikely to grow	Can handle job and has upside potential	Will make big impact. Has quick upside	Will make great impact. 2+ levels upside

Chapter 8

Buyer beware: psychometric assessments, references and other checks

You now have a preferred candidate who has been fully interviewed, and you would like to move forward with an offer. Prior to offer, you definitely need to complete some reference checks (which I'll come to a bit later in this chapter), plus there are some other checks you may want to consider also.

The most important point to make here is that you do not want to make an offer prior to completing your checks, or even make an offer pending completion of these checks (in other words, don't say to the candidate, 'we are going to make you an offer, pending completion of satisfactory references/psychometric/etc.'). Instead, just tell the preferred candidate that you are really pleased with how the process is going, and that the next step is to complete whatever checks you plan to do.

If the candidate pushes back and wants an offer prior to completing the checks, just tell them that this is your process. However, if the candidate wants to get a confirmed salary package or any other condition of the offer that is important to them, before providing referees, this is fair enough. I would not want my referees contacted unless I knew that the employer was going to offer me the salary package I wanted to accept the role.

Psychometric testing

For more senior roles, I highly recommend having candidates complete psychometric testing. There are essentially two types of tests; one type that measures aptitude (for example verbal, numerical and abstract reasoning) and the other profiling personality type.

There are many different types of psychometric tests on the market, from cheap tests completed online through to extremely expensive tests. This includes scenario testing where the applicant comes into an environment where they need to interact with actors, under supervision, to solve a particular imagined crisis scenario.

Like most things in life, you get what you pay for. Cheap online tests in my opinion are not worth the time or money. Firstly, how do you know that the person completing the test is even your candidate? Maybe their next-door neighbour is a genius and they asked them to complete the test on their behalf (that is, they cheated). Also, what environment did your candidate complete the test in? Maybe they were dealing with a sick child, were constantly interrupted by the phone, or had a terrible hangover?

We always recommend that psychometric testing is done under supervision, in a dedicated facility, and that the results are analysed by an organisational psychologist. They can prepare a written report, and can go through the report over the phone or in person with the employer. At the time of writing, this level of testing costs around $1200 in Australia, and in my opinion is a small investment compared to the cost of a poor hire.

Secondly, I do not recommend using psychometric testing as a 'hire/don't hire' decision-making tool. They are not always completely accurate, or alternatively a person may have a particular trait however it is not evident in the test, or it does show up in the test but doesn't affect their work performance. However, psychometric testing should definitely be done prior to reference checks, so that if it indicates any concerning traits, specific questions can be asked of the referees to determine whether it could cause problems.

For example, we were recruiting a CFO and the preferred candidate scored extremely low on their numerical reasoning test (in other words, the test said they were not smart mathematically). This seemed like a bizarre result, given the candidate had a long history as a CFO of some significant and successful businesses. Through reference checks, we were able to confirm that the candidate was very competent, and for whatever reason they had just performed badly on the numerical part of the test on the day.

Another example was a General Manager whose personality test identified them as having narcissistic tendencies and being a poor leader. Through reference checking, we were able to confirm that while they achieved excellent results for their previous employers, they were largely disliked by their teams and peers, and were unable to retain good employees. In this instance, our client decided not to proceed with an offer.

As for supervised scenario testing with actors, I must admit to having no experience with this level of testing. Perhaps if you are recruiting the new CEO of a billion-dollar company you may want to consider this. In my opinion, if you have completed a good performance profile and selected preferred candidates who have 'done it before, done it well, and are motivated to do it again', this level of testing seems superfluous. A good, supervised psychometric test (as I have just described), coupled with high-quality reference checks, should be more than sufficient.

Criminal and financial background checks

Again, for more senior appointments, I would definitely recommend completing criminal and financial background checks. It is especially important when appointing a new CEO for example that they don't have a criminal record or have been bankrupt. How many times do we hear in the media about companies or government organisations appointing a new CEO, only to find out after the fact that they have some major skeletons in the closet? Not a great look for the employer, plus an extremely expensive situation to remedy.

These checks are very inexpensive, usually costing just a few hundred dollars. If the candidate doesn't want to authorise these checks, you have probably dodged a bullet.

Formal qualifications and professional history checks

People lie on their CVs all the time. I actually had a situation many years ago where I interviewed a guy for 90 minutes, and he told me all about his current role with one of my key competitors. His CV and his performance at interview were completely convincing. However, something didn't feel right, so after the interview I rang his 'current employer' and pretended to be someone wanting to speak to him about his services. Not only had they never heard of this guy, but the entire division that he supposedly managed didn't even exist! To say that I was shocked and dumbfounded as to why someone would put on such an act is quite an understatement.

Interestingly, people lie on their LinkedIn profiles far less than they do on their CVs. This is because their LinkedIn profile is in the public domain so people who know them and their career history are much more likely to blow the whistle. As an example, I had an employee I fired after working with me for nine months. He subsequently stated on his LinkedIn profile that he had worked for me for over two years. As soon as it was brought to my attention, I immediately contacted him and said if he didn't change his profile, I would sue him. It was changed within the hour (and then he blocked me from being able to see his profile in the future).

It's also very easy for people to lie about their professional qualifications. In this new age of artificial intelligence, I'm sure getting a fake university certificate of completion would be an extremely cheap and easy thing to do.

May the buyer beware. Investing a small amount of money in getting these checks done, especially if your gutfeel or intuition is telling you something seems off, is a smart investment.

Reference checks

At least two high-quality reference checks, with the candidate's direct past bosses, is mandatory prior to offer. Anyone who hires someone without doing these reference checks is, in my opinion, a moron! Reference checks should not be completed with the candidate's family, friends or colleagues; they should be done with former direct line managers. You may also want to complete additional checks with some customers or subordinates. Remember, you are the potential new employer and you are making a big decision here, so make sure you are entirely satisfied before you make an offer. Feel free to do as many checks as you feel are necessary.

You would think recruitment companies would be the best at hiring practices given this is our profession. Yet I am constantly amazed at some of the terrible choices recruitment companies make with their hiring decisions. Here's an example.

In the early days of Arete Executive, my business partner at the time hired a new recruitment consultant while I was away on Christmas holidays. This consultant was hired through a 'rec-to-rec' (a recruitment company that recruits recruitment consultants for recruitment companies). Not long after this my business partner departed Arete, and I was left to manage this new employee. It became immediately apparent that this consultant was not engaged with his work, was consistently absent, and was not delivering any results.

I spoke with the rec-to-rec and told her I was very concerned about this guy's performance. I asked her to speak with him, and that if he wasn't enjoying working for me, he was welcome to leave. She assured me that she would, and then I didn't hear further from her.

A few weeks later, my level of concern was rising. He was expected to attend a minimum of 10 client meetings per week, and according to his diary and our weekly performance meeting, he confirmed he was achieving this. However, it was not resulting in any new recruitment assignments or positive outcomes. My gutfeel was telling me that something was off, so I decided to investigate by ringing each of the people he said he had had met with in the last two weeks. Needless to say, only two out of 20 said that a meeting had occurred, and for many of the rest, the person did not even exist.

Let's just say that my next meeting with this consultant was heated and resulted in his immediate termination. I told the rec-to-rec exactly what happened so she would be aware of this consultant's behaviour.

Shortly after this, I saw on his LinkedIn profile that he had gone to work for one of my competitors, so I rang his new boss (who I had a good relationship with) and asked her what reason had been given for this person leaving Arete. She told me that the rec-to-rec (the same person who had placed him in my business) told her that I had made this consultant redundant because my business was not travelling well financially.

Firstly, how totally unethical and unprofessional for a recruiter (in this case the rec-to-rec) to lie in order to get a placement fee, even though she knew completely of the circumstances around his termination. But even more shocking is why his new employer did not ring me and ask for a reference. After all, it was clearly on his LinkedIn profile that he had worked for me, plus she knew me.

Not long after this, the consultant was fired from his new employer for faking placements and invoices to get paid commissions for roles that never existed. How much pain would his boss have avoided if she had just picked up the phone?

(By the way, he then left the industry, never to return.)

Reference checks need to be comprehensive and, if at all possible, done face to face or via video call (Teams and Zoom are both great for this). I realise this is not always possible, however there is so much you can learn from the body language of the referee, rather than just the words. I have included our standard reference check form at the end of this chapter.

If you have some way of doing an 'under the radar' reference check (such as with someone who hasn't been provided by the candidate), I think it is reasonable to do so. However, be very conscious of the candidate's confidentiality, especially if they are still employed. If the candidate finds out you have breached their confidentiality, at the very least it will not assist in you in having a good working relationship, plus it could end up with legal action. So unless you can be completely discrete, be very careful.

In this chapter, you have learned:

★ There are many different types of checks that can be undertaken, and depending on the seniority of the role, they are a small investment compared with the cost of a poor hire.

★ Psychometric testing should ideally be done under supervision and prior to the completion of reference checks.

★ Reference checks should be with a minimum of two prior, direct line managers, and conducted face to face or via video call if possible.

★ Other testing includes criminal and financial background checks, and validation of career history and formal qualifications should also be strongly considered.

Reference check template

Candidate name	
Referee name	
Referee title	
Referee company	
Date of reference	
Person completing check	
Position applied for	

Has written consent been obtained from the candidate to perform this reference check?

☑ Yes, proceed with reference check

☐ No, obtain written consent before proceeding

Has verbal consent been obtained from the referee for this reference check, with the knowledge that this information must be passed on to the candidate/referee if requested?

☑ Yes, proceed with reference check

☐ No, obtain verbal consent before proceeding

PLEASE CONFIRM THE FOLLOWING INFORMATION:

Dates employed	
Position held	
Professional relationship with candidate	
Reason/s for leaving	

Include any customised questions

1. What were **the candidate's** key responsibilities and achievements in his/her role?

2. How would you describe **the candidate's** commitment to the role?

3. What do you consider to be **the candidate's** strengths? Why? Could you give me some examples of their key achievements while in the role?

4. Can you give me some examples of where **the candidate** used their initiative?

5. On a scale of 1 to 10, with 1 being the lowest/weakest and 10 being the highest/strongest, how would you rate **the candidate** on the following?

	Rating	Comments
Ability to handle pressure or criticism	–	
Technical competency (computers, software, technical skills required for the role)	–	
Ability to meet deadlines	–	
Punctuality for meetings	–	
Attendance at work	–	
Integrity, honesty and loyalty	–	
Accuracy and attention to detail	–	
Willingness to go the extra mile	–	

ORGANISATIONAL: *Project planning and teamwork abilities*

1. What approach does **the candidate** adopt when planning and monitoring projects?

INTERPERSONAL:

1. How would you describe **the candidate's** ability to work within a team? *(e.g. team player, leader, follower, 'work horse')*

2. What type of environment do you believe **the candidate** works most productively in? *(e.g. busy, structured, entrepreneurial, consistent/steady?)* Why?

3. How would you rate **the candidate's** ability to develop relationships with colleagues as well as with people external to the organisation?

MANAGEMENT: *Best management practices*

1. Describe **the candidate's** relationship with their superiors. How would you describe their ability to take direction and follow through?

2. What type of management style does **the candidate** respond to best? *(e.g. needs strong boundaries, likes freedom and will keep you up to date, constant supervision, nurturing?)*

3. Describe **the candidate's** management style? How did they get the best out of their team?

TECHNICAL: *Problem solving and technical abilities*

1. What approach does **the candidate** adopt when solving a (technical) problem? How effective was he/she in finding a solution? Could you give me an example of the type of problems you observed?

2. Have you observed a time when **the candidate** has had to justify his/her recommendations relating to a (technical) decision/problem? How well did **the candidate** justify his recommendation/decision? What was the result?

3. How flexible is **the candidate** to new trends and new techniques? How does he/she manage these changes?

GENERAL: *Areas for improvement*

1. Can you comment on any areas in which **the candidate** can improve or needs further development?

2. How would you compare **the candidate** to others at the same level you know? Why is this candidate stronger or weaker?

3. Hypothetically, would you re-employ **the candidate**? If so, in what role?

4. How would you rank **the candidate's** overall performance on a scale of 1 to 10? What would it take to move up 1 point? Why?

5. Would you like to add any further comments or observations at this stage?

Thank you

.... *(referee)* we appreciate your feedback on .... *(candidate)*.

Chapter 9

Seal the deal: offer management, counteroffers and employment contracts

You're now on the home stretch. You have a preferred candidate, all your tests and reference checks have come back positive, and you are excited to be making an offer. While after all this hard work getting to a successful hire should now be a 'no-brainer', it is amazing how often things fall over at this point. The two main reasons for this are misalignment on salary and counteroffers.

Salary negotiation

At some point during the various discussions with your preferred candidate their salary expectations would have been raised, whether by you, your internal recruitment team or the external recruitment consultant. Sometimes the candidate may not wish to discuss salary, saying something like, 'I'm more interested in the opportunity than the salary', or, 'let's see if I am the preferred person for the role, and then we can discuss salary'.

To this, I call BS! No one wants to work for free, everyone has a self-perception of their value, and they want to be paid what they believe they are worth. So I always make sure I discuss salary with the candidate in the very first conversation. After all, why waste the candidate's and the employer's time if there is a complete misalignment in salary expectations?

If you are outsourcing the recruitment of the role to an internal or external party, you should insist they ask the candidate for clarity around salary expectations very early in the process. Plus, make sure that the recruiter (internal or external) is skilled at managing expectations (as I discussed earlier in this book) and tells you the truth.

When candidates want a much higher salary than what you are proposing, often less-experienced recruiters either don't want to be the bearer of bad news, or alternatively they expect that at the end of a recruitment process someone will wave a magic wand and the candidate will suddenly reduce their expectations. Let me tell you, this rarely happens, and you are just going to end up with a very angry candidate and line manager, both of whom feel they have wasted a lot of time.

Get clarity around salary expectations early and if these don't match, politely end the dialogue and move on.

What also often happens is that at the offer stage, the employer decides to 'low ball' the salary offer to see if the candidate will accept it. Again, this very rarely works and is quite disrespectful to the candidate, someone you really want to join your business (otherwise, why would you be offering them in the first place?). If the candidate has been clear about their salary expectations, as well as other requirements (such as flexibility or other conditions) at the outset, you should have dealt with these at the time, rather than at the end.

That said, it is a negotiation, and it doesn't mean you should just pay someone whatever they want. Maybe they don't have all the necessary experience, and this may be a 'step-up' role for them, with a resultant lower salary. Maybe they have decided they want other conditions which you would compensate for with a lower salary.

One of the main ways real estate agents justify their commissions is they are able to take the emotion out of the negotiation process when someone is buying a new house. The purchaser typically offers a lower price than the seller is asking for. Buying a house is an emotional process; both parties can get heated and offended, and the sale may fall through as a result. This is why the real estate agent follows a stringent process (usually), meeting with each party individually, as often as required, until the deal gets done.

Likewise, **a quality external recruitment consultant can assist you by taking the emotion out of a salary negotiation.** As an example, a couple of years ago I recruited a new CEO for one of my clients. From the outset, the preferred candidate had told me he wanted a base salary package of $300k including superannuation.

When it came to offer, my client wanted to offer a package that created a greater incentive for performance, with a lower base salary but a higher bonus. They offered a base salary of $200k, however based on the achievement of particular targets, could deliver $400k or greater including bonuses.

When I presented this to the candidate, he was very upset that even though he had clearly articulated his desire for a $300k base plus bonus, he was being taken advantage of. It was highly likely that he was going to withdraw. When I presented this to my client, they were very upset that the candidate couldn't see the upside and was – in their perception – being greedy. It was highly likely they were going to withdraw the offer.

Long story short, through me being able to manage each party's emotions and multiple conversations with each party, we were able to come up with a compromise. The preferred candidate asked for a base salary of $300k in the first year, however with no bonus component. Then from year two, his base would drop to $200k and the commission structure would kick in. Both parties agreed and an offer was made and accepted.

Subsequently, the business performed so well in the first 12 months that had the new CEO accepted the original offer, he would have earned over $500k. I asked him if in hindsight he was upset with his decision, and he said no, it was the right choice for him at the time. The business owners were so delighted with his performance, they kept him on the $300k base *and* included the bonus structure for the subsequent year. A fantastic result for everyone.

So once again, if you are recruiting very senior roles in your business, I would recommend using an external recruiter. The above scenario could have easily resulted in the deal falling through, and the candidate withdrawing. Think of what a lost opportunity this would have been for the employer, given how much success the new CEO ended up bringing to the business.

If you do decide to recruit such a role yourself, make sure there is clarity around expectations early in the process and make sure you can accommodate these. Otherwise you will likely end up wasting a lot of time and damage your Employer of Choice brand.

Counteroffers

You have made your offer to your preferred candidate which they have accepted, an employment contract has been signed, and now they need to resign from their current employer. If your new hire is indeed a top performer, there is a very high likelihood they will be counteroffered to stay in their current role.

Probably my most extreme example of this is when I was recruiting a senior role in the oil and gas industry a few years ago.

We had identified an excellent candidate that my client was excited about employing. This candidate was currently on a base salary of $250k and my client offered them $350k to join. Needless to say, the candidate accepted on the spot.

When the candidate went to resign from his current role, his employer obviously realised they would be losing a very valuable asset, so they offered the candidate $450k to stay. He received a $200k pay rise in one day!

Now it's hard to convince a candidate to walk away from $450k with his current employer, so with my blessing he withdrew from my client's role. That's not to say that my client and I weren't disappointed, however such is life. **We recruiters often describe our jobs as 'champagne and razor blades'** – overjoyed when a placement succeeds, depressed and despondent when it falls over.

It's a common belief in recruitment that 90 per cent of people who accept a counteroffer to stay with their current employer still end up leaving within 12 months. I'm not sure how accurate this figure is, however in my experience the percentage is very high. One of the main reasons for this is that money is only one factor in why a person takes a new role or remains in their current role. Let's remember Lou Adler's 11 factors that candidates use when considering a role and comparing it to their current one:

- Job match
- Job stretch
- Job growth
- Hiring manager
- The team
- The executive leadership team
- The organisation's vision and values
- Tools

- Remuneration and benefits

- Work/life flexibility

- Risk.

Remember from chapter 7 on interviewing, our candidate Sally who is looking for a new job because she feels overqualified for her current role, there's no opportunity for career progression and she is worried the company may be heading for tough times. Note that remuneration wasn't mentioned at all.

Let's say that Sally accepts your role and then is counteroffered with a bump in salary. If your rapport with the candidate Sally is strong enough, you should be able to ask her, 'Even though they have offered you more money, do you still feel overqualified for the role? Do you now have a clear pathway to promotion? Is there still the potential that your current employer is in for some tough times?' In other words, is it just about the money?

This can go a long way towards convincing your preferred candidate to continue with your offer and decline the counteroffer. It's not foolproof, however it is definitely better than just throwing your hands up and walking away. Again, utilising an external recruiter who is skilled at managing counteroffers is my recommendation for more senior roles.

Employment contracts

It goes without saying that when you make a hiring decision and offer your preferred candidate the role, this needs to be followed up with a formal letter of offer and employment contract. If you are the owner of a smaller business and don't have an internal HR and legal team, you definitely want to engage a lawyer who specialises in this area to draw up a contract for you.

I'm amazed at how many employers use an outdated employment contract, or none at all, when making a new hire. Employment law and conditions change regularly so it's important that your contracts represent current legislation. Otherwise you can potentially be facing some significant legal issues and costs if the employee is terminated or makes a claim against you.

I have chosen not to include an example of an employment contract in this book, as I am not a lawyer and you need to get specialist advice. Personally, I utilise a number of different employment contracts for my team, based on their specific role and conditions they are being employed under (for example, are they an employee or a subcontractor? Are they in a sales role or a recruitment delivery role?). I have these contracts reviewed at least every couple of years and amended as required.

In this chapter, you have learned:

★ Always discuss and get clarity around salary expectations with your candidates at the beginning of the recruitment process rather than at the end.

★ 'Low balling' candidates at offer who have been clear about their expectations up front is disrespectful and very unlikely to succeed.

★ External third-party recruiters are able to remove the emotion from a salary negotiation and get a positive outcome.

★ Try to understand a candidate's motivations for considering your role during the recruitment process, to assist you in dealing with counteroffers.

★ Make sure your employment contracts are up to date and comprehensive, utilising an IR lawyer if necessary.

Part II

Retaining top performers

Okay, we're at the halfway point. Thanks for hanging in there. I hope you're having as much fun reading this book as I am writing it.

This next section is where things are going to perhaps get a little bit 'kooky' or 'woo-woo' for you, as I start to explain some fairly esoteric concepts like consciousness, virtues, preferred realities and other topics. Don't worry though, it's all going to come together in a system for managing a high-performance culture and retaining top talent that has not only worked for me, but has also worked for the many CEOs, business owners and senior executives I have coached over the years.

Most of these frameworks were taught to me by my coaches and mentors and I have endeavoured to acknowledge those people throughout this book. They in turn have taught these models to their vast numbers of clients over the years, so I feel completely confident in saying that if you read, understand and most importantly implement what you are about to learn into your business, you will be stunned at how quickly high performance will ensue.

Retaining top performers

Chapter 10

A brief segue to chat about consciousness

A false view of reality

As mentioned in the introduction to this book, my own personal journey has been very much one foot in a traditional, Western business context (business degree, MBA, corporate career, starting a business) and the other foot in a more metaphysical, Eastern spiritual context (four years living in a Buddhist monastery, extensive meditation and other retreats, training as a psychotherapist).

I've certainly found the Eastern teachings I've had the great fortune to learn have been extremely beneficial to my professional career, plus have allowed me to coach senior leaders in a unique way. What I'm going to attempt to explain in this chapter is how to view consciousness, and in particular our own unique consciousnesses (yes, I just checked and that's actually a real word). It might seem like I'm going off on a decidedly 'woo-woo' tangent, however bear with me. All will be revealed soon, young Grasshopper.

Every single one of us, from the time we were born until now, has been taught a false view of reality. In fact, I'd suggest that 99 per cent of people reading this book still believe this false view, as it is perpetuated in almost every aspect of our lives. Once you understand the truth it becomes completely obvious what is true, and knowing this truth makes life (and leading teams) so much easier. (Note that I'm not saying that we have been told lies for any nefarious purpose, just that it's a misunderstanding of the way the world works.)

Jed McKenna is one of my favourite authors on this subject, and I highly recommend his very unconventional and thought-provoking books, starting with the Enlightenment trilogy. His writing has helped me to clarify and galvanise my own thinking on this subject.

So what is this false view of reality?

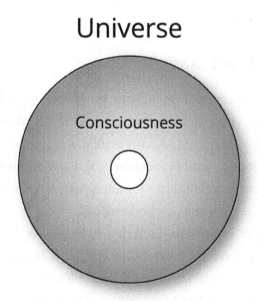

We all are led to believe that we each have a unique, individual consciousness, that exists within a universe that is outside of us, and is the same for all of us (see the illustration above). We each go about our lives, doing our thing, operating within a shared universe. A shared universal experience.

However, what is actually true is that **we each experience our own unique universe, that exists within our own unique consciousness** (see illustration below). That's right, each of us is experiencing our own unique universe. These universes can be vastly different and can in fact even oppose the universe another person is experiencing (sometimes even to the point of violence – just think about the conflicts between Russia and Ukraine, or between Israel and Hamas. In both instances two different groups of people with completely contradictory views of the universe, and therefore lives experienced).

Consciousness

Universe

Let me give you a couple of examples:

Example one: Friend, Enemy, Stranger

In Buddhism, there are lots of amazing meditations that are offered as a way of teaching certain concepts. In my four years of intensively studying Buddhism, I found many of these meditations extremely enlightening. This one is called 'Friend, Enemy, Stranger'.

Let's say Bill is walking down the street and he sees me standing on the other side of the road. Bill thinks to himself, 'There's my great mate Triggsy. Gosh he's an awesome bloke. I really enjoy his friendship. Look at his incredibly handsome beard. I can't wait to say hello to Triggsy'. Bill crosses the road, grabs my attention and we have a fun conversation.

Because Bill is seeing me through the lens of 'friend', he sees aspects of me he is attracted to. His feelings literally determine how he physically sees me in a positive light.

On the other hand, let's say Belinda is walking down the street and she sees me standing on the other side of the road. She thinks to herself, 'Uungh, there's that idiot Richard Triggs. Gosh he's a loser. I can't believe anyone would like him. Look at that scruffy beard. I dislike him so much I'm going to pretend I haven't seen him so I don't need to speak to him'. Belinda keeps her eyes down and hurries past.

Because Belinda is seeing me through the lens of 'enemy', she sees aspects of me she is averse to. Like Bill, her feelings literally determine how she sees me in a negative light.

Finally, Steve is walking down the same street and sees me standing on the other side. Steve has no idea who I am and has never seen me before. To Steve, I am a 'stranger', and he barely pays me any attention. In fact, I probably don't even appear in his consciousness.

From my side, I am neither friend, enemy nor stranger. I'm just Richard, standing on the street. However, from Bill's, Belinda's and

Steve's perspectives I appear completely differently, based on their beliefs about me and how they feel about me. **I will literally look different to each one of them, as experienced within their own unique universe.**

Example two: coffee anyone?

It's Monday morning and I'm walking down the street to my office in town. As I walk past my favourite coffee shop, I can smell the spicy, delicious aroma of freshly brewing coffee. My eyes light up and my mouth begins to water in anticipation of my first, sensational coffee of the week. I'm literally joyously excited to drink this amazing 'nectar of the Gods'.

Sally on the other hand hates coffee. She can't believe anyone could possibly drink, let alone enjoy that vile muck. As she walks past the coffee shop, the smell is like an olfactory assault. She virtually holds her nose as she rushes past to keep out the stench.

Anna has just started a new job and is new in town. She grew up in a Mormon household and community that never drank coffee, so she has literally never smelled freshly brewed coffee before. She wonders why there is a long line of people waiting to get a hot drink, however she doesn't really pay it any attention.

Once again, you can see that three people are having a completely different experience because of their belief about coffee. From passionate desire, through ambivalence to abject rejection, just based on opinion. Objectively the coffee smells the same for everyone (or does it?), yet each person's experience is completely unique.

The universe does not exist as some objective, uniform thing that is 'out there'. The universe for each of us is experienced 'in here' (within our own consciousness) and as such is completely unique to each of us. It makes complete sense once you think about it, doesn't it?

The universe is reflective, reflexive and determined by intention

Okay, so now that I have bent your brain exploring consciousness a little, the next step is to think about how each of us create, maintain and indeed even change the universe we are uniquely experiencing. Again, these insights date back to ancient philosophies. This time we are going to go back to 1 AD and the teaching of Hermes, called the Hermetic Principles or the Kybalion.

A couple of years ago I started working with a psychotherapist, Adrian Luus. Adrian is one of the best psychotherapists I have ever worked with and learned from. I've referred well in excess of 50 CEOs and business owners to Adrian and all have had life-transforming experiences. Adrian talks about these Hermetic Principles extensively in his work and I learned much about this from him.

The first Hermetic Principle is 'All is Mind'. This is what I have just illustrated. The universe we each experience is ultimately created in our mind (or consciousness). We each have unique minds, and as such experience unique universes.

If we accept this as true (which I hope you do), there are three key elements that allow us to firstly understand, and then manipulate, the universe we experience:

- The universe is **reflective**: If my mind creates my universe, the universe I am experiencing is a 'reflection' of my state of mind. How is it that two people, with the same opportunity and environment, can have two vastly different experiences? One experiences joy and happiness, while the other experiences sorrow and angst (I'm sure we all know people who fall into both categories). Our state of mind is the precursor to the universe we experience.

- The universe is **reflexive**: If I change my state of mind, the universe 'flexes' accordingly. Why do we love stories of redemption, like Uncle Scrooge in *A Christmas Carol* who went from being a greedy, lonely miser to a generous, loveable man? How about stories of the phoenix rising from the ashes, where failing businesspeople or sportspeople or celebrities or everyday people are transformed from poverty or failure to tremendous success? Joseph Campbell's *The Hero's Journey* documents how these stories have existed throughout history. Change your mind, and the rest will follow.

- And it all comes down to **intention**: If we want to create substantive and lasting change, we need to change our intention, and therefore where we put our attention. By keeping our attention on what we want (rather than what we don't want), the universe will re-flex and reflect our preferred reality.

At this point, you are probably wondering, 'What on Earth is Richard going on about, and what has this got to do with attracting and retaining top performers?' Don't worry, I'm laying the foundations for how you are going to build awesome teams. Really.

The three states of consciousness

Right, we now know that 'All is Mind', we each are experiencing our own unique universe, and the universe we are experiencing reflects our state of mind or where we are putting our attention. Now let's explore the three different states of consciousness we experience. You will have heard of at least two, if not all three of these before.

Conscious

Humans are conscious beings, right? Many believe that it's our consciousness that has allowed us to evolve beyond other animals. We live our lives consciously – walking, talking, working, loving, eating. In essence, we are having a conscious experience of consciousness.

While this is definitely true, why is it then that – for most of us – we don't always get what we want? If I was to walk down the street and ask 100 random people what they want, most would say something along the lines of, 'I want to be healthy, wealthy and happy.' Yet if I was to ask them if they were as healthy, wealthy and happy as they would like, most would say, 'No'.

If All is Mind (consciousness) and I am conscious, if I want to be healthy, wealthy and happy it should just happen, right? So what's going on? What is the glitch in the Matrix? Oh ... it's the dreaded subconscious.

Subconscious

While we think we are conscious and going about our days in a conscious way, it's actually the subconscious which is really driving our behaviours. The subconscious mind is incredibly powerful, many believing it is far more powerful than our conscious mind. For example, according to Dr Bruce Lipton, author of *Biology of Belief*, the subconscious mind is 500,000 times more powerful than the conscious mind.

Colin Clerke, another former coach and great friend of mine, frames it like this. When we are born, we come into the world as a blank canvas (let's leave any consideration of souls, reincarnation and other beliefs out of this conversation). As a very young child, we start to observe the world and develop beliefs about how the world operates, and how we should operate in order to be successful. Our primary role models in developing these beliefs are our biological parents, assuming they are both on the scene. If not, then the other significant adults in our lives.

Our parents have their own beliefs about the world, which over the course of their lives have become patterns that are enacted subconsciously in daily life. Often these patterns are less than optimal and create a degree of dysfunction, from absent parenting right through to abusive relationships. Some examples of these negative beliefs are:

- Anyone who is wealthy must have ripped someone off.

- All bosses are assholes.

- Anyone who is different from my tribe (race, religion, appearance) can't be trusted.

- If I want to be loved, I need to be a good girl/boy and not speak up.

- I need to be aggressive if I want people to take me seriously

- I can't succeed no matter how hard I try.

As a young child, typically up until the age of seven, we have very limited capacity to know the truth of these situations. We make up stories about why our parents behave in certain ways. Colin refers to this as our 'wounding'. Then, as we grow up, we look for evidence that what we believe is true (remember, the universe is reflective), and these beliefs become even stronger and cemented in our subconscious.

Speaking personally, as a 55-year-old adult man, I can consciously say to myself that I want to eat less and exercise more. I consciously know the probable health consequences of my largely sedentary lifestyle, plus I want to look and feel better. Consciously, I know exactly what I need to do to regain my health and wellbeing.

So why do I continue to eat and drink too much and exercise too little? I'm not a lazy person, I'm not depressed, and I'm not ignorant. Yet my poor diet continues because of certain beliefs I made up about the world as a small child through my experiences with my parents. These beliefs became subconscious patterns I still carry today.

This is not to say that I in any way blame my parents. I could not have hoped for a better upbringing. My parents loved me, there was always food on the table, and I felt safe. Food equated to love and safety, so now my subconscious says that if I want to feel safe and loved, I should eat, drink and be merry. And thus, the pattern continues.

This is where tools like psychotherapy can be extremely beneficial. If you are not experiencing the life you would love to live, exploring your beliefs and subconscious patterns can often shed light on what is really going on. Once you become clear on what patterns you may be subconsciously enacting, you can choose to take a new course of action (remember, the universe is reflexive, and it all comes down to intention).

Likewise, every person you interact with in your life, including all your employees, has their own subconscious patterns of behaviour that substantially affect how they interact with you, their work, and all other elements of their lives.

Superconscious

This is where the magic happens. This is where you create what you would truly love. Think about it this way. Nothing has even existed in the physical world without having existed as thought previously. This computer on which I am writing this book existed in the inventor's mind before it became a reality. This house in which I am writing this book existed in the mind of the architect before it was ever built.

The superconscious is the place of dreaming and visualisation. Not in some 'woo-woo, hippie-dippy' way – the best creators know how to harness their superconscious to bring their dreams, and their lives, into reality.

If I know there are subconscious patterns that are holding me back from living the life I would love, then rather than trying to break the pattern (which is virtually impossible after 55 years of life) I instead harness my superconscious, through intention and attention, and start consciously creating.

The reticular activating system

The final piece of this consciousness puzzle that I want to discuss is the reticular activating system (RAS) and its role in where we put our attention, and as a result, the universe that we experience. The RAS is a part of the brain that essentially acts as a filter. We are constantly bombarded with thousands of sensory inputs every moment of our lives through our senses (sight, smell, sound, taste and touch). If we were conscious of all these inputs at all times it would be completely overwhelming.

One of the RAS's jobs is to sort through all these inputs and only allow those which are important to us to get through to our conscious awareness. The easiest way to understand this is through an example.

A few years ago I decided I wanted to buy a new car. I did some research online, I visited a few car yards, and I spoke to a few friends to get their opinions. The car I decided to buy was a Volvo XC60 (I am over 50, after all). At the time, it had won some awards, and I was surprised that I hadn't seen them around much on the road. So I thought I was buying a cool car (well, as cool as a Volvo can be I suppose), and one that was also a bit rare.

No sooner had I bought my Volvo, I started to see them every-where. It seemed like every time I went for a drive, I would see at least one on the road or in a carpark. I started seeing them in movies, on billboards and in magazines. Suddenly this unique car wasn't so unique after all.

Now the reality is that these Volvos were always there. It's just that my reticular activating system did not know they were important to me, so they were filtered out of the information that got through to my consciousness. Once the RAS knew I was interested in Volvo XC60s, it started to draw my attention to what was already there.

Why is this important in the context of this book? Firstly, as stated earlier, the universe is reflective, reflexive and determined by intention (or where we put our attention). So if we start to consciously put our attention on what we want, the RAS will become programmed to identify and highlight these sensory inputs. People often refer to this as 'synchronicity' or 'co-incidence' (the coinciding of events), which can also sound a bit 'woo-woo'. A more scientific explanation is that the RAS is just doing its job.

The other reason why this is important is that you cannot assume that what is important to you is important to someone else. How many times have you thought to yourself, *Why can't this person understand what I'm talking about? It's so obvious. Are they a moron? Am I speaking in a different language?*

Understand that if their RAS does not think that what you are saying or demonstrating is important, the person literally can't see or hear it. Until their RAS is congruous with your message, it can't get through. It's not that the other person is a moron, they just have a different filter.

Unless the RAS is programmed consciously, our subconscious is driving the show. Our subconscious is looking for evidence that confirms our belief patterns are true, so our RAS filters out information contrary to this.

You can be the most generous, supportive and encouraging boss, however if your subordinate's belief pattern is that 'all bosses are assholes', all they will see, hear or feel is the negative. Their RAS is doing its job perfectly, even though as their leader it is completely misaligned with your intentions.

Okay, let's now bring all this information together into a methodology for driving a high-performance culture and supporting your team members to achieve their highest potential.

In this chapter, you have learned:

★ Each of us is experiencing our own unique universe, which is created in our own unique mind (or consciousness).

★ This universe we are experiencing is reflective, reflexive and determined by our intention (or where we are putting our attention).

★ Although we believe we are experiencing our lives consciously, our subconscious and superconscious both also play important roles in our lives.

★ The reticular activating system also plays a critical role in our own lives, plus in how we communicate (and miscommunicate) with others.

Chapter 11

The fish rots from the head down: setting the tone from the top

There is a saying in recruitment, 'people join companies; they leave bosses'. Employees are attracted to organisations because of their brand and reputation. In my experience, the number one reason employees choose to proactively look for another job is because of their boss. From a perceived lack of leadership or poor rapport right through to a hostile relationship, people mainly quit their jobs because their boss pisses them off!

Of course, as in all things, there are two sides to every story (the subordinate's view of the truth, and the boss's view of the truth). Regardless, as leaders it is imperative that we create and maintain a workplace where we are beyond reproach. If we are truly committed to attracting and retaining top talent, the last thing we want to do is jeopardise this by behaving in a way contrary to our goals.

I've certainly worked in environments where the behaviour of the executive leaders has been appalling. From being sexually inappropriate, to excessive drinking, workplace bullying … I've seen it all firsthand, as many employees have. As a recruiter, the stories I have been told over the years by candidates about the toxic environments they have worked in would fill a book on their own.

Plus, if I am completely honest, I look back on some of my own behaviour as a leader and know in hindsight there were times that I could have, and should have, done better. I'm sure most people reading this book would feel the same.

The Four Cardinal Virtues

As mentioned earlier, a couple of years ago I started working with a psychotherapist, Adrian Luus. Adrian introduced me to a concept called the Four Cardinal Virtues, which was originally credited to Plato and then later expounded upon by Aristotle.[4] In essence, the Four Cardinal Virtues are a structure, or guide, as to how we can lead a virtuous life. I have found them invaluable from a leadership perspective. They are:

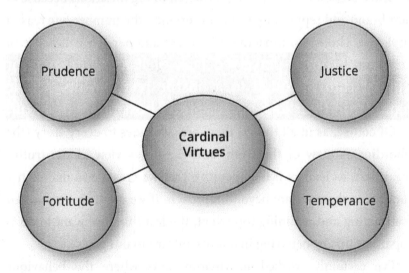

---

4   https://plato.stanford.edu/entries/plato-ethics/

Prudence

The first Cardinal Virtue is prudence, which in this context Wikipedia defines as 'the ability to discern the appropriate course of action to be taken in a given situation at the appropriate time, with consideration of potential consequences'. One could also view prudence from the perspective of being prudent in one's dealings with others, or in speaking one's truth.

You have probably heard the expression, 'don't cast your pearls before swine'. Why not? Because the swine (pigs) will just gobble them up, not realising how valuable they are.

So firstly, think clearly about the ramifications of any action you are considering and its consequences for your team. Also, **think clearly about who you share your truth with**. Do they have the mental or emotional intelligence to understand and manage that information appropriately?

Too often leaders take team members into their confidence without considering what the downsides of doing so are. When in doubt, err on the side of silence. 'Loose lips sink ships' and the consequences of prematurely or inappropriately sharing your thoughts with the wrong people can be disastrous.

Justice

Justice refers to being just in your dealings with others, as you would expect them to be just with you. Are you engaging in office gossip or judging people without giving them a fair hearing? Do you truly honour and value your employees, their lives, their goals and aspirations? Do you speak positively and encouragingly at all times?

Every person in your team has a right and desire to be dealt with justly. As their leader, I'm sure you expect them to deal justly with you. To show up for work on time, give 100 per cent effort, support the goals of your organisation, and behave safely and ethically. Are you reciprocating accordingly?

Fortitude

For me, fortitude in the context of the Cardinal Virtues has two distinct meanings. The first is wishing good fortune for others, as you would wish it for yourself. Do you truly wish good fortune for your staff, your customers, suppliers and other key stakeholders? Are you consistently communicating this through what you say, and more importantly how you act?

Employees are not dumb, and they are judging you by your actions, whether you like it or not. As an example, are you paying your creditors within their payment terms? Do you speak ill of former employees who have left the organisation? Do you disparage your competitors unnecessarily or without evidence?

The other aspect of fortitude is how we look after ourselves. Think about when the Romans invaded a country, or the American soldiers moved into Indigenous territories. One of the first things they would do is to build a fort. By having a safe, enclosed space they could protect their troops and plan their strategies.

As Adrian likes to say, 'if you look after the constitution, the government will look after itself'. In this instance, what he's referring to is our personal health. If your constitution is healthy (the body), your government (your mind) will be much more effective. Are you looking after yourself well? Are you eating a good diet, exercising regularly, and getting enough sleep? Your employees are looking at you, and yes, judging you, based on how well you treat yourself. Who wants to work for a boss that is tired, grumpy and unhealthy?

With the goal of personal transparency and vulnerability, this is my main area requiring attention. Due to a couple of serious injuries, Covid, the ending of a personal relationship, and generally being excessively busy, my own health has suffered a lot. I've put on a lot of weight and gotten into bad habits around diet, exercise and sleep. At 55, I know I need to deal with this and that I am being judged based on my appearance. It's time for me to take action, and maybe for you too?

Temperance

The final Cardinal Virtue is temperance, which, according to Wikipedia, is 'restraint, the practice of self-control, abstention, discretion, and moderation'. In the context of leadership, it's important to realise that there will be days when you will be hot (angry or grumpy) and there are days when you will be cold (distant or withdrawn).

It's only natural, and indeed important, that we feel the full range of human emotions. Stuff happens in our personal and professional lives that affects our moods. We are not robots, and our staff don't expect us to be. Some days we are on white, and other days we are on black.

However, if I am feeling hot, it's important I don't burn people. If I'm feeling cold, it's important I don't freeze people out. This is where the practices of restraint and self-control become important. Maybe work from home that day, or let people know in advance how you're feeling so they can give you some space. Again, we are all only human and your team will appreciate your vulnerability and honesty.

So as I hope you can see from this brief introduction to the Four Cardinal Virtues, upholding these virtues will assist you greatly in attracting and retaining staff. However, it's not easy and requires us to be brutally honest with ourselves every day.

A good practice is to end each day by doing a review:

- What did I do well today?
- What could I have done better?
- Would my team be proud of me as a leader? Why?

If you don't think your team would be proud of you that day, rather than beating yourself up, just make a plan as to what you can do better tomorrow.

In this chapter, you have learned:

★ The Four Cardinal Virtues is a great framework for ensuring that our behaviour as leaders is above reproach, which is essential for retaining our top performers.

★ Prudence: be careful who you share your truth with.

★ Justice: treat your team and all those you come into contact with justly, as you would expect them to do to you.

★ Fortitude: prioritise your health and wellbeing.

★ Temperance: be careful not to burn people, or freeze them out.

Chapter 12

The King and the Jester: a leadership parable

In 1994, I was working for P&O Services in a sales role. I'd been with the company for about a year and had done my first sales visit to Cairns in Far North Queensland. I immediately fell in love with the tropical environment and the fantastic people I met there. At the time I was riding motorcycles and I thought riding the coast road from Cairns to Port Douglas, then up through the ranges to the Atherton Tableland and Kuranda, was heaven on Earth.

A couple of months after my visit, the local manager in Cairns resigned, so I immediately went to my boss Peter King and asked if I could take it on. I was 26 years old and had never managed anyone in my career. I was asking him to take a gamble on me to take over managing a team of approximately 140 people, with no relevant experience. Fortunately for both of us, Peter offered me the job and we worked successfully together for many years (a big shout out to Peter if you are reading this book).

Prior to me packing up my belongings and heading to Cairns, Peter told me a story about the King and the Jester.[5] I wonder whether Peter even remembers this story, however for me it was and remains one of the greatest lessons about leadership I have had in my career. Here it is.

The King and the Jester

One evening, after court had concluded for the day, the King and the Jester sat together and had a beer, prior to heading home. They had known each other for a while and had become friends, at least as friendly as a King and a Jester ever could be.

The King said to the Jester, 'You must have the most fantastic life. All day you get to have fun and play, making people laugh. It must be awesome to be so carefree. My job as the King really sucks. Everyone takes me so seriously all the time. I just want to be able to relax, let my hair down and have a good time, but everybody is too scared of offending me.'

The Jester replied to the King, 'It's actually really terrible being the Jester. Yes, I get to have fun and make people laugh. However, nobody ever takes me seriously and I can never get people to listen to me or do what I want.'

So the King and the Jester decide to conduct a little experiment and switch jobs for a month, to see what it was like on the other side. At the end of the month, they caught up again for a beer after court had ended for the day.

The King said to the Jester, 'How did you enjoy being the King?' to which the Jester replied, 'It was terrible. Yes, I got to wear the crown

---

5   I know in the brave new world of gender equality and inclusion, the King could equally be the Queen or even the non-binary Monarch. You may even be against traditional societal constructs like having a monarchy and instead want to use 'Supreme Leader'. So for simplicity of storytelling, I'm using the word King, however you are welcome and encouraged to use whatever word you choose to. With love, Richard

and robes and sit on the throne every day, however every time I tried to get people to take me seriously, they would just laugh and say they knew I was just the Jester pretending to be the King. Nobody gave me any respect.'

The Jester then asked the King what it was like being the Jester for a month. The King said, 'It was fantastic. I had so much fun, and everybody really enjoyed my company. However, if I needed to say anything serious, they would still respect me and do as I asked, because they knew I was really the King.'

What's the moral of this story, you ask? Start hard and then get soft. Too often leaders step into a new role and start by trying to be everybody's friend. How often do you hear newly appointed leaders say that for the first 90 days they just want to observe and build a friendly rapport with their team?

While it's true you don't want to start out like a bull in a china shop, and break things prematurely, you definitely want to immediately and conclusively create a relationship with your team where they respect you as their leader. You want to be friendly, but not friends. People want to be loved, and they also want to perform. Your obligation to them is to create a high-performance environment where they can excel and achieve their highest potential.

Thank you, Peter King, for this valuable lesson in leadership. I have shared this story countless times during my career and it has served me incredibly well in my own leadership journey.

In this chapter, you have learned:

★ Start hard, and then get soft.

★ Be friendly, but don't be friends.

Chapter 13

Can you have your cake and eat it too? The fine balance between love and accountability

One of the greatest challenges that leaders have to face is how to build and maintain a high-performance culture that is sustainable. We want to retain our top performers, so our inclination is to provide a nurturing atmosphere that creates lots of space and freedom for people to do their best work. Yet when we do, performance often suffers, and subsequently we lose good people.

Likewise, we may find ourselves in a situation where we have an excellent performer, however they don't play well with others. We want to retain these people to get the benefit of their skills and experience, however the consequence is that the broader team becomes dysfunctional, and we subsequently lose good people.

Who said this leadership and retention stuff was easy, huh? What should we do? Here's a couple of models I have found very helpful.

Love versus performance

You want to create a culture that is loving and that also encourages high performance. The challenge is that if our culture emphasises being a 'lovefest', all 'unicorns and rainbows', without sufficient emphasis on performance, the culture becomes soft. People become accustomed to underperforming, they see their peers underperforming, and this lack of performance becomes endemic and 'business as usual'. People who want to perform become demoralised and leave. This is more often seen in owner-led businesses where the boss is uncomfortable having tough conversations.

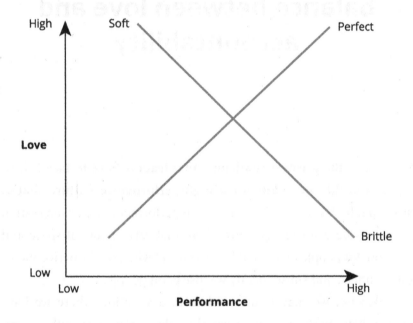

On the other hand, a culture that emphasises performance but is not loving enough becomes brittle. Staff feel underappreciated and undervalued, thinking the boss only cares about the bottom line. High performers become self-interested and are more likely to chase another job with better conditions for themselves. This is often seen in larger corporates with a strong emphasis on financial metrics or KPIs, rather than a more holistic view of organisational health and performance.

The trick becomes maintaining a balance between ensuring the team are feeling the love, while also having clear performance expectations. People want to feel loved, and they also want to feel successful. We will be spending quite some time later in this book understanding how best to achieve these two complementary goals.

Cultural fit versus performance

Here's another model which is useful for considering culture versus performance, in this case on an individual level, when determining whether to retain somebody or not. I first saw this model at a workshop presented by my great friend Tim Dwyer, Founder and CEO of the Tolemy Group. Tim is a fantastic brand strategist and has worked with many of my clients.

Cultural Fit

	Low	High
Performance High		
Performance Low		

Let's say you have someone who is both a high fit culturally and is a strong performer. They are in the top-right quadrant. What should you do? Of course, you would want to retain them in the business, because they are exactly the kind of people you want to employ.

Let's say you have someone who is a poor culture fit and a poor performer. They are in the bottom-left quadrant. In this instance, the obvious action would be to terminate them.

Now it becomes a bit trickier. What about someone who is a great cultural fit, however a poor performer? The team love them, they love the company, however they just aren't doing a good job. What should you do? An often-overlooked solution is to retrain this person for a different job, one that they will be competent in. This will allow you to retain a great advocate and team player. Too often poor performers are terminated without considering this option.

Now for the final quadrant, the toughest one of all. You have a great performer, who achieves excellent results, however is a poor cultural fit. The team doesn't like working with this person, it's affecting morale, and there is a high likelihood their ongoing behaviour will result in the loss of other good employees.

What should you do?

The most likely outcome is that you need to terminate them. You can call them out on their behaviour and demand they improve the way they interact with others, however it's highly unlikely this will result in lasting and positive change. There's no denying that this is a tough call to make, however for the maintenance of a sustainable, positive culture that balances love and performance, these people have to go.

Reviewing each member of your team regularly is a good habit to get into, assessing their performance and cultural fit and taking early remedial action if and when required.

In this chapter, you have learned:

★ Finding the right balance between love and accountability is the mark of a great leader.

★ People want to do what they love and are good at, plus they want to be held accountable.

★ Employees who are strong performers, but a poor fit culturally, generally need to be terminated for the good of the team (and the business).

Chapter 14

Onboarding: the first 90 days

Getting off on the right foot

Today is an exciting day. All that hard work finding and securing your new employee has paid off. We're going to call this new employee Sam for the rest of this book, to keep things easy.

Almost certainly there has been a period of time between the hiring decision and signing of employment contracts, and Sam's actual commencement date. This could even be up to a few months, depending on Sam's resignation period and/or need to relocate for the role.

Make sure everything necessary is put in place prior to Sam's commencement date. There is nothing more frustrating for new employees than coming to work on their first day and not having the tools they require in place (for example, a computer set up and ready for action). Make sure there are meetings already scheduled to introduce Sam to relevant key stakeholders both internally and externally. Make sure any induction requirements are scheduled and can be completed promptly so Sam can get to work.

You want Sam's first day to be a great experience. You want Sam to feel completely at ease that she has made the right decision to join your organisation and she is excited about the future. These first impressions are critically important, and yet are often handled poorly.

(I once placed a CEO in a not-for-profit. He needed to relocate interstate with his wife to a regional town to take up his new role. When he arrived for his first day of work, there was no one from the board there to greet him. His staff were not expecting him and there wasn't even a desk prepared for his arrival. It was a disaster. Needless to say, he was completely underwhelmed by the whole experience and ended up resigning from the role within six months.)

Sam has now arrived, and everything is ready to go. This is your first opportunity to establish your relationship with her. Remember to be the King and not the Jester. Start firm and then soften. Ensure from the very first moment you are managing that balance of love and accountability well.

How do you do this from the very beginning?

Remember that performance profile you developed for the role at the beginning of your recruitment process which clearly articulated the desired key deliverables of the role over the first three, six and twelve months? This performance profile was shared with Sam during their recruitment process, and Sam had provided sufficient evidence that she had 'done it before, done it well and is motivated to do it again'. Otherwise, you wouldn't have hired her, would you?

In other words, Sam has complete clarity over what is required during her first 90 days of employment. What you are going to do is set up a regular formal meeting (I'd suggest in the first 90 days this should be at least weekly) and in that meeting the first point of business is to **refer to the performance profile and ensure that these**

early tasks are being achieved. Once again, Sam is expecting this so there should be no surprises.

Here's an example from a performance profile I used in my own business, Arete Executive, when hiring a new General Manager.

First three months:

- Induction and training in systems including Outlook, Vincere, Zoom, Teams and LinkedIn Recruiter, etc.

- Induction and training in recruitment methodologies.

- Induction and training in sales process.

- Get to know all staff – build rapport, establish reporting relationships.

- Run weekly team meetings, plus individual team 1:1s.

- Attend client meetings with Richard, either face to face or online, to take over existing relationships and learn how to develop new relationships (goal to be self-generating a minimum of 12 client meetings per week either face to face or online within three months).

- Attend a minimum of one Sounding Board meeting and one Brisbane Long Lunch Club.

- Fill a minimum of two roles as Associate Partner to learn our recruitment process.

- Bill sufficient revenue from recruitment activities as Senior Partner/Associate Partner to cover base, from roles largely won by Richard and then handed over.

- Strategically review current product and service offerings and recruitment processes and make any recommendations for changes.

For the first 90 days, at every one of your weekly meetings you will check with Sam that each one of these tasks is on track to being achieved comfortably within the allotted timeframe. You are seeking feedback from Sam as to whether she has any queries, questions or concerns. You are proactively offering your feedback and support (the love), and even more importantly you are setting up a relationship of demanding performance (the accountability). You are the King, you are firm, you are friendly, but you definitely aren't friends.

My friend Colin Clerke refers to this as being like making a cake. The ingredients of the cake are placed into a bowl in order to be mixed. The ingredients are soft; however the bowl is hard and rigid. In this metaphor, the bowl is the KPIs or key deliverables. As the baker (the leader) your role is to massage the ingredients gently and competently within the firm structure of the bowl. If there is no bowl (no structure), it's impossible to make the cake.

A mistake leaders make regularly (and I've certainly been guilty of this myself in the past) is to appoint someone and then go soft on the KPIs from the beginning (if they are even referred to at all). Sam starts, and early in her appointment she makes some excuses as to why she is not achieving the early goals required. You cut her some slack, because after all, she is new, right? We don't want to be too demanding, because it took a long time and cost a lot of money to recruit Sam, right? We don't want her to get upset and quit, right?

In my own leadership experience and having seen this hundreds of times when recruiting for organisations, this almost always ends in disaster. If in the early days you accept a lack of performance (after all, you are the boss), it's extremely hard to get things back on track. Remember, people want love, and they want accountability. It's your job to make sure that from the absolute beginning you are setting up this dynamic appropriately.

Of course, there can be extenuating circumstances that mean some of these first 90-day goals may need to be reviewed. Maybe priorities have changed, or certain things may require a longer timeframe. You have hired a person, not a robot, and their feedback and opinions are important and should indeed be welcomed. So like most things in life, common sense should prevail.

'Hire well, and fire fast'

I imagine most people reading this book will be familiar with this saying. Yes, we all try to hire well (after all, why would you intentionally hire poorly?). Yet for most leaders, we don't fire nearly as fast as we should. I once persevered with someone in my business for three years, even though I knew within three months that he was a poor hire. I got him executive coaches, I implemented new systems and structures to accommodate him, I put my own needs secondary to trying to retain him because 'he'll come good eventually'. Three years later he resigned, and I realised I'd been through three years of absolute frustration and disappointment for nothing. If only I'd trusted my intuition and fired him in the first three months, my life would have been so much easier.

Why do we do this? Why don't we learn our lesson?

I watched a great short video recently by Gary Vaynerchuk, and I think he absolutely nails it.[6] What Gary says is that it's our own ego which stops us from firing fast. After all, we are great at hiring, aren't we? So if we fire someone fast, doesn't that mean that we're *not* very good at hiring in the first place? Our egos don't like to admit we are wrong, so we persevere with a poor hire rather than making the right decision.

---

6   Here's the link, however note it does include some saucy language (like me, Gary enjoys the occasional swear word): www.youtube.com/watch?v=-r8zKoNx_YA.

One of my greatest lessons in business, one which I constantly share with my clients and friends, is that if in the first three months you don't see a complete commitment to performance and the values and culture of your business, it is imperative you fire that person. A moment of pain is definitely worth the long-term gain.

In this chapter, you have learned:

★ Make sure everything is prepared for your new employee's start date the moment they arrive.

★ Refer regularly to the key deliverables in your performance profile to make sure things are on track.

★ Establish from day one your absolute expectations of accountability and performance.

★ When in doubt, make the tough call and fire fast.

Chapter 15

Current reality versus preferred reality: a framework for ongoing performance management

We are now moving into the crux of this entire section on how to develop and retain high performers (and thereby high-performance teams). Let's start by examining a framework first taught to me by Colin Clerke. I'm going to bring into this all the preparatory work we have done in understanding consciousness and the other models mentioned previously.

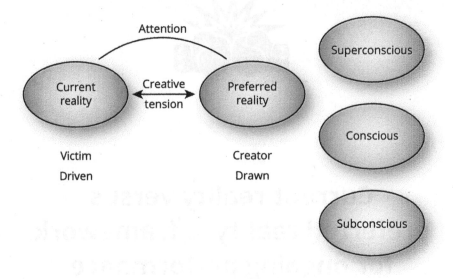

Let's start by defining the terms I use in this model.

Current reality

Each of us exists within our own current reality. This is our own personal universe that we are experiencing. You could view this fairly broadly (for example, I'm a 55-year-old man, business owner, father of two, living in Brisbane, Australia) or you could view this more specifically in relation to a certain aspect or attribute of your life (for example, I'm 20 kilograms over my preferred weight).

Preferred reality

As the name describes, this is the reality (or universe) we would prefer to experience. Again, in my example I could say that my preferred weight is 20 kilograms less than what it is currently.

Each of us has a preferred reality, which is different from our current reality, unless you are someone who truly exists in the moment and has no desires at all. Having lived in spiritual communities and met many of these so-called 'enlightened' individuals, I would say this state of Samadhi (no desires or aversions) is an illusion.

You might want better health, more money, six-pack abs, a gorgeous life partner, better-behaved kids, a new job, more work/life flexibility, world peace … The options are endless, and we all have desires.

You can never exist within your preferred reality; you can only exist within your current reality (thus the name). There will always exist a gap between current reality and preferred reality, although over time this may become more subtle as you largely achieve the life you'd love to live.

Creative tension

Once you have determined your preferred reality, and understand your current reality, this creates a tension between the two. This is not to be understood as a negative tension (like stress), but more like a structural tension. If you can imagine holding a rubber band between your two hands (one hand representing current reality and the other preferred reality), as you stretch your hands apart the rubber band comes under tension. Eventually this tension must resolve itself in one of two ways. Either your current reality is drawn towards your preferred reality, or your preferred reality collapses back to your current reality.

Attention

Referring back to the earlier chapter, the universe we experience is reflective, reflexive and determined by where we put our intention (or attention). If we want to achieve our preferred reality, we need to keep our attention on this. However, if we keep our attention on our current reality (on what we would *not* prefer), that is the universe we will continue to experience.

If most of us want to be 'healthier, wealthier and happier' than we currently are (our preferred reality), why aren't we experiencing this? It's because we are continuing to keep our attention on what we don't want.

Why do we do this?

Victim

People who remain stuck in their current reality often have a victim mentality. This is not to say they are being a victim in the way it's commonly portrayed ('I'm a victim, everyone hates me, the world is out to get me ...'). In this context, it means there are things people want, but they can't have them because of circumstances they see as beyond their control. Some examples:

- 'I would love to be 20 kilos lighter, however I can't because my job requires too much client entertaining, eating and drinking too much.'

- 'I would love to have better-behaved kids, but I can't because my partner is a poor parent.'

- 'I would love to start my own business, but I can't because I have to pay the mortgage and kid's school fees.'

- 'I would love to have "X" (my preferred reality), but I can't because of "Y" (circumstances outside of my control).'

Creator

On the other hand, people who are able to move towards their preferred reality do so because they have a creator mindset. They accept responsibility for their current reality (responsibility = the ability to respond). Through accepting responsibility, they understand they have at least co-created their current reality (co-created because sometimes things happen which are outside of our control).

If I at least co-created my current reality, that means I can also create the life I would love to live (my preferred reality):

- 'If I want to lose 20 kilos, I either make better food choices at events or entertain less frequently.'

- 'If I want to have better-behaved kids, I either get my partner to share this goal or I end the relationship.'

- 'If I want to start my business, I either do so part-time while still working or I sell my house and move my kids out of private schools.'

Life is all about choices, and rather than blaming our current reality on 'circumstances outside of our control', we can make different choices and create the life we would truly love.

Driven

For people who remain stuck in their current reality, often this is due to having goals that they are *driven by*, rather than *drawn to*. They make choices based on what they think society wants, their parents want, 'keeping up with the Joneses' and other similar beliefs. Goals that we are driven by are hard, they take effort, and they aren't fun.

Countless times in my career as a recruiter I have heard senior executives say that they have worked so hard, for so many years, and sacrificed so much for their careers, only to find that they hate their job, they feel disconnected from loved ones and their health has really suffered. They have 'climbed the ladder, only to find it was leaning against the wrong building'.

Drawn

On the other hand, people who are able to move towards their preferred reality do so because they have goals they are *drawn to*, rather than *driven by*. If we are creating the life we would love to live, we are drawn to that life. These goals are energising, easeful and fun. It's a pleasure to get out of bed each morning and go out and achieve them.

In our Western culture, having a mid-life crisis is perceived as a bad thing, often negatively portrayed as the man who buys a sportscar and has an affair with a young co-worker, or the woman who leaves her family and responsibilities to take on a new life somewhere else.

However, the more traditional Eastern view of a mid-life 'crisis' is actually a positive thing. The belief is that for the first half of our lives we are obliged to do what society would have of us – become educated, get a career, have a family and be a dutiful provider. Once we reach our mid-life (our 40s to 50s), we have fulfilled our obligations and are now free to make new life choices that we are drawn to.

What is the life that you would truly love to live?

Conscious

As previously discussed, we believe that we are consciously living our lives and making conscious choices about our preferred realities and what actions we need to take to achieve them.

Subconscious

Again, as previously discussed it's actually our subconscious that is driving the show. Those early beliefs from our childhood which have become subconscious patterns of behaviour are what can stop us from achieving the goals we consciously want. For most of us, these patterns go uninspected (unless you are using tools like psychotherapy and other modalities), and so we have no idea why we can't achieve our goals. It's incredibly difficult as we get older to shift or remove these old patterns that no longer serve us. However, by becoming aware of them, we can catch ourselves when we slip into these old beliefs and proactively make different, more preferable choices.

Superconscious

This is the space of dreaming and visualising what we truly want. In other words, making it up. Remember, nothing can exist in our tangible reality without having existed as a thought in our minds first.

Most business professionals are very competent when viewing their current reality. Spreadsheets, business plans, P&Ls and balance sheets are rooted in current reality. Yet most businesspeople find it hard to, and have had limited training or experience in, consciously 'making up' what they want (at a superconscious level).

Action

Of course, we can't simply make up what we want at a superconscious level and then wave a magic wand and 'hey presto!', our brand-new Mercedes-Benz appears in our driveway, or the love of our life walks in our front door. Unlike what some movies and self-help books would have you believe, deliberate and concerted action is required to create our preferred reality. We need to 'keep our heads in the clouds (superconsciously make it up) and our feet on the ground (take action)'.

This is where the magic happens, the secret sauce, that will strap a rocket to your team member's performance and success in your business. True and sustainable high performance comes from encouraging your people to dream and then holding them accountable for the actions required to realise those dreams. That beautiful balance of love and accountability.

Putting it into action

Let's look now at how you put this into action, using a story as an example.

Why can't most leaders delegate well?

I don't know about you, but delegation for many leaders seems to be their Achilles heel. They know they need to delegate more to be able to create the time to focus on higher order, strategic tasks. They also know that to develop their leaders of the future, they need to groom them by providing tasks that will stretch their people. So it makes excellent sense to delegate, right?

Yet one of the biggest fears that leaders can have in delegating is the person they delegate to mishandles the task or needs lots of handholding, which creates more problems than it's worth. So the leader ends up thinking to themselves, 'Oh well, I may as well just do it myself. If you want to get something done, give it to a busy person (blah, blah).' How many times have you thought this yourself? I know I have, too many times to count over the years.

Let's analyse this problem within the Preferred Reality model I've just been discussing.

Mary (the leader) feels she is overworked and not able to fully achieve the goals of her role. She wants to be working at a more strategic level. Her boss (the CEO) also wants Mary to take on a new project, which will increase her workload even more. Mary has a competent team, and her **preferred reality** is that she can delegate more tasks to her subordinates.

When she assesses her **current reality**, she determines that while her team are competent at their daily tasks, she has not really given them much opportunity to prove themselves with more complex priorities. Mary has been keeping a tight handle on these larger priorities because she always wants to do a good job and receive positive feedback from the CEO. She hasn't trusted her team to do these things well. However she also knows that unless she starts to delegate effectively, she won't be able to advance in her own career much further.

Mary engages her **superconscious**, visualising her life with a highly functioning team. She can take on these exciting new projects, get promoted to a more strategic role, and stop working ridiculously long hours trying to get everything done. Mary is excited and looking forward to the future.

We now have a **creative tension** between what Mary wants (to delegate well) and what she currently has (an unproven team, at least in relation to these tasks). Mary starts to take **action** by selectively allocating a few of these tasks to certain members of her team and instituting a reporting system to make sure the tasks are on track.

A few weeks have gone by, and things seem to be going well. Early indications are that the tasks are being performed competently and the milestones are being reached. Using the rubber band metaphor from earlier, the creative tension is being eased as Mary is drawn towards her preferred reality.

However, a few small issues have started to arise. Mary is getting a bit worried and is starting to question herself. She starts to see evidence that she has made the wrong decision. She's still keeping a close eye on the KPIs (which are being achieved) but in her mind her team are starting to drop the ball. She starts to micromanage more and becomes more controlling.

Mary has started to move her **attention** from her preferred reality back to her current reality. And Mary's universe (which exists in her consciousness) re-flexes and reflects what she doesn't want.

Suddenly there's a big problem: a key outcome is not met, and a major client complains to the CEO, who subsequently holds Mary accountable. The CEO is not happy, and Mary hears it loud and clear. Suddenly Mary's 'relaxing rubber band' comes under massive tension again.

What happens? Mary's attention is now fully on what she doesn't want. Mary throws her hands up in the air, admits defeat and then takes the tasks back on herself. The delegation plan is scrapped, and things go back to the usual. Mary's entire attention has been pulled back to her prior, less desirable, current reality.

Mary's **victim** statement: 'I can't trust my team. If I want something done well, I have to do it myself. I should have known this was too good to be true.'

Mary's **driven** statement: 'Do I actually want a promotion anyway? Maybe I should just stick to what I'm good at? My job requires 70-plus hours a week – I just have to accept that's the way it is.' (Believe me, I hear this stuff from senior executives all the time, plus have said these things to myself in the past.)

If we stare into the future, the probable outcome is that Mary will burn out and resign; her team will never achieve their own potential; and the organisation will suffer as a result. I'm sure the CEO doesn't want any of this.

What could Mary have done differently? Well, she had a preferred reality that was important to her – more interesting work, a potential promotion, more free time as she worked fewer hours, a more competent team. There were lots of benefits to achieving these outcomes.

At a **conscious** level, Mary made the choice to start delegating, and she put in some systems and KPIs to keep things on track. She was initially excited about this project, and it started well. Yet at the first sign of trouble, she immediately put her attention back on her prior current reality (what she doesn't want) and old beliefs.

Remember, the universe is reflective, reflexive, and it all comes down to where you are putting your intention. Remember also that it's actually the subconscious driving the show. Perhaps Mary's mum and dad had certain beliefs about the world around trust and work that Mary subconsciously chose to take on. Maybe she had some traumatic experiences when she trusted someone and felt they failed her. Maybe later in her life she had some experiences in her career where problems arose, and she was left 'holding the ball' and needing to do everything herself.

(Of course, we can't psychoanalyse our employees or even suggest that they should do so themselves. Doing that work is very personal and can be highly confronting, so people will only generally look at their subconscious patterns of behaviour if they have a major traumatic event or if they are genuinely curious and/or wanting to achieve their highest potential.)

What Mary could have done is – the moment she felt her attention going back to her negative thoughts about her current reality – put her attention back intentionally and proactively onto her preferred reality and re-engage her superconscious. One of the best ways to do this is to actually write your preferred reality down and consciously visualise yourself having achieved your goal, ideally every day. Then, when you perceive things as getting a bit wobbly, it's much easier to break your fixation on what is wrong.

Note that this may seem simple, but it's not easy, especially if we have highly ingrained patterns of behaviour. It can take tremendous effort to break these habits of looking for what is wrong and keeping our attention on what we would prefer.

Mary's **creator** statement: 'I have created this situation now where things seem to be going off track. I'm still highly committed to achieving my preferred reality, with a team I can delegate to with complete trust. What systems or KPIs do I need to change?

Who should I consult with? Should I ask the CEO for help? What else can I do to achieve this great outcome?'

Mary's **drawn** statement: 'I'm so excited about my future life and all the wonderful possibilities once I have achieved this goal. I will leave nothing to chance, and nothing on the table. I'm going to achieve this goal with the support of my team and CEO, no matter what!'

It's our job as business owners and leaders to support our employees in achieving their goals and full potential. It takes time and effort to institute an effective system which enables this, however it's definitely worth it. So let's get on with the job, shall we?

In this chapter, you have learned:

★ Each of us has a preferred reality, where we have things or attributes that we don't have in our current reality.

★ The gap between these two realities creates a structural tension that must be resolved.

★ Often when we don't get what we want, it's because we have a victim mentality and/or goals that we feel driven to.

★ People who are able to achieve what they want typically have a creator mentality and goals they feel drawn to.

★ We need to keep our attention on what we do want and take the necessary actions to create it.

★ Our subconscious can interfere with our ability to get what we want, through ingrained self-limiting beliefs that have become patterns of behaviour.

★ Recognising this, our role as leaders is to support our subordinates to 'make up' their preferred reality (the working life they would love to lead) and then hold them accountable to the actions required to achieve this.

Chapter 16

Implementing a high-performance culture through love and accountability

Let's use our new employee Sam to illustrate how to successfully implement the framework I've described so far. I will break out from time to time to look at the bigger picture.

Sam has now been working for you for three months. Early indications are excellent; she has achieved the key deliverables identified in the performance profile, she has built a strong rapport with both internal and external stakeholders, plus you are enjoying working with her.

While the performance profile did identify key deliverables for both six and twelve months, no doubt since Sam has been appointed some of these priorities may have changed, plus Sam will have used this period to come up with her own ideas about key priorities and how to deliver them. However, if there are some non-negotiable key deliverables from the original performance profile, these should definitely remain in place.

Three months is an appropriate time to implement the model we have been discussing. By this time, Sam has gotten her feet under the table and gotten to know the lay of the land. Moving into the Preferred Reality model immediately with a new employee may be counterproductive, as they 'don't know what they don't know' yet. If they are part of a larger team, they are probably hearing this language anyway, so it won't come as a surprise to them.

Of course, it's entirely up to you as to whether you decide to move to this model earlier than three months, however I definitely would not recommend delaying it any later than that. Again, this is about being the King, not the Jester, and creating that fine balance of love and accountability. Getting into the preferred reality groove post the initial induction phase is critical to its success.

'What are the three reasons you love working here?'

This is a great question to ask each member of your team regularly and consistently. I would recommend you ask this question of each of your subordinates at least once a year. Ideally, this question should be asked face to face directly by the line manager rather than HR.

'Sam, I really appreciate you working here. You could have the opportunity to work anywhere, and so I'd like to ask you, what are the three reasons you love working here?'

You will be amazed at how varied and interesting their answers are, plus how surprised you may be by the person's answers. Really listen to what they say. Common responses include:

- 'I love the team I get to work with.'

- 'I love the interesting variety of projects I get to work on.'

- 'I love the flexibility to work from home.'

- 'I love the vision the company has.'

- 'I love our clients and helping to solve their problems.'

- 'I love working with the latest technology.'

- 'I love being mentored and supported.'

- 'I love the pay.' (Nothing wrong with this.)

Note the choice of language is really important – 'why do you <u>love</u> working here'. Why? Because you want people to love working for you. If they don't love it, as their leader your responsibility is to either change the environment or role or tasks so that they do love it, or politely and graciously exit them from your business.

Of course, if you are giving them what they love, the law of reciprocity is that they should give you what you love – a highly functioning team member who is committed to achieving the key deliverables of their role and your organisation.

Don't be afraid of the word *love*, because at the end of the day that's what we are all looking for and deserve. 'Love is all you need' (come on, sing along with me …).

Exploring a preferred reality

'Sam, you've now been working here for three months. What I'd like to do now is discuss your vision for your role in the future. Let's imagine it's six months from now (make sure you use an exact date, for example 27 September). What I'd like you to describe is what your role would look like if you were really proud of what you have achieved. I'm not talking about it necessarily being absolutely perfect, but just for you to be really pleased with the results.'

What you are doing here is engaging Sam's superconscious. She is starting to visualise ('make up') her preferred reality. You want to get her talking about what would make her truly happy, getting into as much detail as possible and writing it down. Note that you are not looking for what she is going to do at this stage (the actions required), you are just exploring the bigger picture. You want to get her excited.

Let's say Sam is your Sales Manager. Here's an example of what she might say:

- 'We have grown revenue from $1m to more than $2m per quarter.'
- 'I have employed two new salespeople to replace the two that are underperforming.'
- 'We have a strategic plan in place to launch our products internationally within 12 months.'
- 'We have won another two ASX top 50 clients.'
- 'You are so happy with my performance, you agree to pay for me to do an MBA.'

If Sam's goals align with your own and the business, this is fantastic. She is taking ownership of her own vision of the future, rather than having it dictated by you. As a result, she will take greater responsibility and accountability for seeing it delivered (you'll see how we achieve this in a minute).

However, let's say that Sam's vision is out of alignment with yours. Maybe your sales target is a lot higher, or you disagree with a few of the other goals. Here is your opportunity to discuss it and either get Sam's agreement, come to a compromise, or make the decision that Sam needs to exit. Remember, it's your business, and Sam needs to fit in with your preferred reality.

What I have found interesting doing this exercise hundreds of times over the years is that the employee (Sam) is more likely to set goals that are too high and unrealistic. Again, it's our job as their boss to bring them down to reality.

So we might say, 'Sam, I think two ASX top 50 clients within six months is unrealistic, given the long lead times we have for making a sale. How about we say instead that we have four active prospects within six months and have two sales agreements in place within 12 months?' Sam will appreciate your wisdom and guidance, plus have a sense of relief that you have a lower expectation.

Current reality

Sam has now created her preferred reality, and it has been documented and agreed upon by both of you. The next step is to get her to become clear on her current reality and determine the steps required to achieve this. So what you say is, 'Sam, what I want you to do is imagine it is now the 27th of September (the date six months from now). The exact date at which you will have achieved your preferred reality. Imagine yourself standing there and looking back six months to today's date. What I'd like you to do is describe the *specific actions you took* to take you from where you were six months ago (today's date) to now (27th of September).'

I get that this seems a bit weird, however the language is really important here. Once again, you are looking to engage Sam's super-conscious. If instead you were to say, 'Okay Sam, so how are you going to achieve those goals?', then Sam is looking at the situation from within her current reality paradigm. By getting Sam to imagine herself in the future looking backwards instead of forwards, she is 'making it up' within the context of her preferred reality. It's what my friend Adrian Luus refers to as 'mental gymnastics'.

When Sam starts to describe the actions she needs to take, it's important to make sure they are specific, measurable and within a certain timeframe. This is where the accountability comes in. So as an example, Sam might say:

- *Goal one: Revenue growth from $1m to more than $2m per quarter.*
  'Within the first month I have analysed each of our clients based on potential for increased sales volume and reallocated these clients across the sales team to those most likely to drive revenue growth. Each team member will have specific KPIs that I will then measure weekly to ensure targets are being met.'

- *Goal two: Employ two new salespeople to replace the two that are underperforming.*
  'I will immediately start performance management of the underperforming team members to ensure we can terminate without potential legal action. I will reach out each week via LinkedIn to three potential new salespeople, with the goal of having one introductory meeting per week and then hire when appropriate.'

- *Goal three: Win another two ASX top 50 clients.*
  'Within the next month I will map each of the ASX50 companies, identifying the key decision maker/s for our product. I will personally look after these companies and start a regular call cycle. I will arrange five meetings per week so I have met with all the companies within 10 weeks. I will then present a comprehensive sales strategy to the board based on my findings and identifying where we should best be investing our attention.'

What you want to do is align each goal with specific, measurable actions that can be reviewed on a weekly basis in your formal meeting with Sam (these meetings can become less frequent over time). You then say to Sam, 'Okay, that's fantastic. What I am going to do is document these in a table. And then every week when we meet, the first thing we are going to discuss is the numbers. That's okay with you, isn't it?'

Of course, Sam has to say yes because she came up with these goals (preferred reality) and then she came up with the weekly action tasks required to achieve these outcomes. Once again, if you think the weekly tasks are not appropriate (for example, Sam says she is only going to meet with one ASX50 company per month), this is your opportunity to discuss it and either get Sam's agreement, come to a compromise, or set a different goal instead.

You also need to ask Sam what assistance or support she requires from you to achieve these targets. If reasonable, make sure you are fulfilling your responsibilities proactively so that there is no possible comeback from Sam if she does not fulfill her responsibilities.

Sam – Key Performance Indicators (next quarter)

Goal	Week (Goal / Actual)											
	1	2	3	4	5	6	7	8	9	10	11	12
1. $2m/qtr revenue target:												
Complete analysis of existing clients				COMPLETE								
Allocation to sales team				COMPLETE								
Commenced KPI measurement				COMPLETE								
Revenue target / week	($84k /)	($84k /)	($84k /)	($84k /)	($167k /)	($167k /)	($167k /)	($167k /)	($167k /)	($167k /)	($167k /)	($167k /)
2. Appointment of new salespeople												
Performance management of existing team	Commenced	Update	Update	Update	Update	Update	Update	Update	Update	Update	Update	Update
LinkedIn approaches / week	(3 /)	(3 /)	(3 /)	(3 /)	(3 /)	(3 /)	(3 /)	(3 /)	(3 /)	(3 /)	(3 /)	(3 /)
Initial meetings with prospects	(1 /)	(1 /)	(1 /)	(1 /)	(1 /)	(1 /)	(1 /)	(1 /)	(1 /)	(1 /)	(1 /)	(1 /)
Successful hire (anticipated)						1						
3. Win two ASX50 clients												
Map key decision makers				COMPLETE								
Meetings with key decision makers					(5 /)	(5 /)	(5 /)	(5 /)	(5 /)	(5 /)	(5 /)	(5 /)
Present sales strategy												Due in 2 weeks

As you can see in the table opposite, Sam's KPIs have been included for the three example goals. You provide Sam with a copy of the table and ask her to enter the week's results prior to your weekly meeting.

You must make the numbers the very first item on your weekly meeting agenda. You want Sam to clearly understand that this is the minimum accepted performance. You will not accept Sam not bringing her numbers to the meeting, and you definitely will not accept underperformance.

You are the King, not the Jester. Your rule is *law*! Remember my analogy of baking a cake. The KPIs are the rigid bowl that creates the structure within which you mix your ingredients. Make sure you have an excellent, impervious bowl.

This performance management style will work for any role in your business. Obviously, the goals and activities will be vastly different for a finance manager versus a human resources manager, however the principles remain exactly the same.

How it plays out

Let's look at some examples, so you can get a feel for how this management style typically plays out.

Managing poor performance

I'll continue with the sales theme and use as an example my own business, where my Senior Partners (client-facing salespeople) are expected to meet with employer clients to win and deliver our recruitment assignments. A pretty typical goal is 10 to 12 meetings per week once they have been working with me for three months.

The following dialogue is almost exactly what happened in my business with my most recent hire. I'm certainly not sitting in an ivory tower trying to convince you I'm perfect. I have made some very poor hiring decisions in my career, and this is just the latest one. Fortunately I now get it right far more often than I get it wrong.

Week one:

Richard: 'Okay Fred, as you know, last week you set your accountability goals and determined you were going to do a minimum of 10 meetings per week. So let's look at the numbers. How many meetings did you have last week?'

Fred (name changed to protect the not-so-innocent): 'Well … ahhhh … I only did three, but they were really good ones!' (looking for praise).

Richard: 'I'm glad they were good ones, and you can tell me all about them in a minute. However, you said you were going to do at least 10. What prevented you from achieving 10?'

(Never ask 'Why?', as this generally results in the person making up a reason. By asking 'What', 'Who', 'Where' and 'How' you are much more likely to get a more honest answer and something that you can work with.)

Fred: 'The dog ate my homework'; 'the cat got stuck in a tree'; 'my car broke down'; any lame excuse for poor performance. If the excuse is genuine, of course you want to help them solve it. After all, you have invested a lot of time and money in recruiting, training and inducting Fred.

Richard: 'Okay, however we have agreed that the minimum target is 10. You still agree that this is the target, correct?'

Fred: 'Yes, boss, I'll definitely have at least 10 meetings this week.'

Richard: 'Okay, let's move on.'

Week two:

Richard: 'How many meetings, Fred?'

Fred: 'Well … ahhh … Only four meetings.'

Richard: 'What precluded you from achieving your minimum target of 10?'

Fred: (Lame excuse.)

By now, Fred is starting to get pretty nervous. Fred doesn't enjoy underperforming and he definitely doesn't enjoy sitting in front of me every week and being put under the spotlight.

Week three:

Richard: 'How many meetings, Fred?'

Fred: 'Three.' (gulp).

Richard: 'Fred, I really like you as a person, otherwise I wouldn't have hired you. However, I'm starting to feel that either you can't or don't want to do this job, or alternatively you think I'm an idiot. Which is it?' (Then shut up and hold the silence for as long as necessary until Fred replies. Silence is a very powerful tool.)

Fred: 'I'm sorry, I just don't think I'm a good fit for Arete Executive and I should resign.'

Richard: 'Fair enough Fred. I wish you all the best.'

Occasionally the underperformer, faced with such consistent and unrelenting scrutiny, will lift their performance to an acceptable level and go on to be a successful member of your team. However, in my experience this is very unlikely, and holding onto the belief that 'they'll come right' rarely pays off.

Remember, hire well and fire fast. However, if the person chooses to resign, how much better is that? No unfair dismissal claim, the person can leave with some dignity, and you've just removed someone who, quite honestly, is stealing from you – not just their salary, but also your time and emotional health. Get rid of them, pronto!

I've been using this performance management framework for almost 20 years, and I have never once had an unfair dismissal claim. As the old saying goes, 'give someone enough rope and they will hang themselves'. These meetings are documented through recording the stats (KPIs) plus notes taken after the meeting. Coupled with the fact that the employee set their own targets and signed off on them, it's very hard for them to present a valid unfair dismissal claim.

Leadership through coaching

Sometimes your team member may have a valid reason for not meeting their KPIs and/or they are losing faith in themselves to actually succeed in the task. As their boss, if you feel the situation can be remediated and you really want this person to succeed, it's your responsibility to coach them to success rather than just criticise their performance.

To do this, you need to directly intervene and get the person to remember to keep their attention on their preferred reality, rather than focusing on their current reality. Using our earlier example of Mary who wants to delegate successfully, if the CEO had been meeting with her weekly and looking at the numbers (or however they had chosen to measure success), at the first sign of a problem the CEO could have intervened like this:

CEO: 'Mary, remember how excited you were when you came up with your goal of delegating more effectively? Remember how great you felt about achieving your preferred reality and the wonderful benefits that would come from this?'

Mary: 'Yes, but ...'

CEO: 'Mary, where are you currently putting your attention? On what you *do* want, or what you *don't* want?'

Mary: 'Yes, I see what you are saying. I'm already starting to doubt myself, doubt my team, and I'm preparing to take these tasks back on myself. I'm focusing on what I don't want.'

CEO: 'Okay, so let's focus instead on what needs to happen to make sure you achieve your preferred reality. What needs to be done, and what can I do to help you?'

The CEO now moves into coaching mode. This conversation needs to be repeated every week if necessary until Mary is back on track, or a decision is reached to remove Mary from the project or role.

Managing strong performance

Let's now look at a much more positive, and definitely more common, situation. You have hired a top performer, because you hired someone who has 'done it before, done it well, and is motivated to do it again'. So them performing excellently is far more likely than underperforming.

People like to do what they are good at. They like to achieve their goals, impress their boss, be praised and held in high esteem. Who doesn't want to feel loved?

Week one:

Richard: 'Okay Steve, as you know, last week you set your accountability goals and determined you were going to do a minimum of 10 meetings per week. So let's look at the numbers. How many meetings did you have last week?'

Steve: 'I had 12 meetings. Some of them in hindsight probably weren't worth my time, however it was a great opportunity to practice my pitch.'

Richard: 'That's fantastic Steve, a really great effort. Let's discuss how you can perhaps be more discerning about who you choose to meet with in the future.'

Week two:

Richard: 'How many meetings, Steve?'

Steve: 'I only did 10 this week, however they were much more productive, and I've already been asked to submit three new proposals.'

Richard: 'Steve, you are a superstar. Let's work on those proposals together.'

And so it goes. Excellent performers are worth their weight in gold. They love to achieve, and they love to be praised. Make sure you shout about their accomplishments in team meetings, give them opportunities to share their wisdom, and reward them richly.

But – don't stop measuring the numbers. Keep up this discipline, even if you think they don't need it anymore. What doesn't get measured doesn't get done. Perhaps just change the things you measure, as your team members become more skilled or take on more strategic responsibilities in your business.

Every three months, sit down with each team member and set a new preferred reality for six months' time. What of their existing goals and activities need to be changed based on the previous three months' experience? Perhaps there are certain tasks that even need to be stopped?

Also, this tool is not only for new employees. Start to implement it with every one of your direct reports, and then train your direct reports to implement it with their direct reports, and so on. This tool is extremely effective for all employees whose roles involve setting and achieving certain outcomes.

Of course, the forklift driver's or office receptionist's jobs may be far more mundane, however even they want to do well and be appreciated for it. So set some suitable goals, measure their performance, and praise them for achieving excellence. It's such a wonderful and easy way to manage people, once you get the structure right and the discipline to implement it consistently and well.

In this chapter, you have learned:

★ Find out why each of your employees specifically loves working for you, and then keep giving it to them.

★ Get your employees to engage their superconscious and 'make up' their preferred reality, and the actions necessary to achieve it.

★ Meet weekly to review their progress (via clear KPIs) to instill clear and effective accountability.

★ Make sure when they achieve their KPIs you praise them frequently and publicly.

★ Never accept underperformance – either remediate through coaching or terminate.

Chapter 17

Performance managing teams, managing up, and managing external stakeholders

Hopefully by now you have seen what a fantastic tool the Preferred Reality model is for managing your team members and supporting them to achieve their highest potential. The great thing about this model is that it is equally applicable and effective in managing all your professional relationships (not to say you can't also use it for personal relationships, although you may want to tread carefully when trying to performance manage your intimate partner or mother-in-law … Just saying).

Let's have a brief look at each of these various stakeholders in a bit more detail.

Managing teams

The logical extension to managing an individual's performance is managing the team in which they operate. It's actually a fun and engaging way to harness the full team into achieving team-based goals and/or taking remedial action.

As an example, I once coached a CFO who had taken on a new position, where one of the critical key deliverables in the first three months of their employment (as stipulated in their performance profile – remember those from earlier in the book?) was to break down the silos between the finance team and the rest of the business.

This was a major performing arts company and there was no current engagement between the finance team and the core business. Put simply, the finance team under the previous CFO had not been encouraged to interact with the 'artists' in the company. As a result, the finance team felt isolated, and the rest of the business felt their needs were largely ignored. (This is also often the case in businesses where sales and operations feel in conflict. The operations team blame sales for overpromising, and the sales team blame operations for underdelivering. I'm sure most readers have experienced this during their careers.)

The new CFO was able to engage their team in creating a new preferred reality vision for the finance team. Within six months the finance team wanted to feel excited about working with the rest of the business, be seen as a real contributor to the broader success of the company, and to have developed strong and positive relationships with their 'artist' colleagues.

When they developed their action plan, each finance team member took responsibility for attending performances in the future (this hadn't happened previously). They allocated specific internal key stakeholders to each member of the finance team, who they would reach out to proactively and ask what they could do to be of greater service, and then bring this feedback back to the team. They subsequently discussed the feedback and put in action steps to address each point.

The results were immediate and extremely positive. Suddenly the attitude from the broader business towards the finance team became that they were 'highly valued', 'great team players' and even 'fun'. Needless to say, this was a great win–win for everyone, and the CEO and board were delighted with the CFO's performance.

Managing up

I work with many senior leaders and a common complaint is a lack of consistency in direction from their boss (or chairperson) and/or a lack of clarity about what is required of them to succeed in their role. Perhaps they want a promotion or pay rise, but don't have clarity about what is required to achieve this. Or they may actually be in conflict with their boss about achieving a specific outcome.

Once again, the Preferred Reality model is an excellent tool for getting you and your boss on the same page and focused on achieving the same goals. Let's use another example.

I was coaching a CEO who worked for a private company, owned by two brothers. While in the early years of the business the two brothers got on well and worked together excellently, in more recent years their relationship had fractured to the point where they were in conflict about the direction of the company. One brother wanted to pull as much money out of the company as possible to fund his lifestyle, while the other brother wanted to keep reinvesting profits for future growth into new products and markets.

Their conflict extended to their personal lives, with neither brother wanting to spend Christmas or other important family events, like their children's birthday parties, together. It was a stressful time for everyone. A major motivation in recruiting a CEO was to have a more skilled and experienced person to drive the business into the future.

It wasn't long after the CEO was appointed that he came to understand that the conflict between the brothers was not only a distraction to achieving the goals of the business, it was also having a significant effect on the overall morale of employees who were witnessing hysterical arguments in the workplace. Some highly valued employees resigned, and retention was becoming a real issue. Plus the CEO was constantly being drawn into meetings with each individual brother, trying to recruit him to their side of the argument. It was untenable and the CEO was already thinking strongly about exiting.

Almost at his wits' end, the CEO asked me for advice, and I told him to have a 'come to Jesus' meeting with the two brothers, lay his concerns on the table, and work towards building a new preferred reality that would accommodate the two brother's individual desires plus allow the CEO to get his job done in peace.

When asked to describe their preferred reality, one brother admitted he had lost his passion for business and wanted to essentially take his money, exit, and enjoy an early retirement. The other brother was still excited for the future and derived a lot of his self-worth from being the owner of a highly successful and profitable business. The CEO's preferred reality was to be empowered to deliver the results he was employed to achieve, and to be able to do this without interference or conflict.

The brother who wanted to retain ownership was unable to pay out his brother immediately, so the agreed vision was that within two years there was sufficient capital to enable this to happen. When they focused on the action steps to take, they came up with the following:

- The brother who wanted to exit would move to a non-executive director and shareholder role and not actively work in the business any more.

- An independent chairperson would be appointed to support the CEO and help to mitigate any future conflicts between the brothers.

- The CEO would start to investigate and then engage a corporate financial consulting firm to put in place a plan to find an external investor to buy the first brother out.

- Both brothers agreed to only meet with the CEO jointly at a monthly board meeting, and to no longer have hostile conversations within the workplace.

The result was a far more harmonious workplace, retention significantly improved, and the CEO was able to deliver excellent results. Within the two years, the business achieved a much higher valuation than was originally anticipated and both brothers were delighted with the outcome. Needless to say, their personal interactions at family events were far more positive and they returned to enjoying a loving relationship.

Managing external stakeholders

Imagine entering into a major agreement with a new supplier, client or strategic alliance partner. Imagine that you are currently in conflict with one of the above. Think of the opportunity cost should the relationship fail or not achieve its full potential. Think not only of the financial cost to your business, but also all the time wasted that you and your team, plus the other party, have invested.

What if at the beginning of each new relationship, or alternatively at the first hint of a dispute, you sat down with their key people and together built a shared vision for the future, a shared preferred reality? Each party then commits to action steps they will take, and also how you will each hold the other party accountable, in a positive and constructive way. **What an absolutely fantastic way to ensure you are all communicating effectively, and jointly contributing to each other's success.**

It does take some time to set up these agreements, plus you may get some initial pushback from the other party, however it's definitely worth it. And if the other party doesn't want to participate, maybe you shouldn't be in business with them anyway?

In this chapter, you have learned:

★ The Preferred Reality model can be utilised across all of your professional (and even personal) relationships.

★ Teams can set collective goals, assign individual tasks to each person, and hold each other accountable.

★ Disputes or frustrations with your boss can be easily resolved through clear communication about your expectations of each other and a shared vision for the future.

★ Agreements with external stakeholders can be far more successful with a clear agreement on what you are hoping to achieve together.

Chapter 18

What is your preferred reality?

guess you knew this was coming. How can you hold other people to account unless you take your own medicine? I don't know about you, but I seem to be much better at critiquing other people's performance than my own. Somehow, I always seem to find a loophole or 'get out of jail free card' when it comes to myself. This is why having an external coach can be extremely valuable. I always have at least one external coach, and for the last few years I have had two, one for my personal/mental wellbeing (Rex Urwin) and a business coach (Andrew Griffiths).

I mentioned earlier that I first learned the Preferred Reality model from my great friend and master coach, Colin Clerke. Colin has now retired from coaching and is enjoying a wonderful life near Byron Bay. He coached me and members of my team for many years, plus I referred him to many of my clients.

I achieved extraordinary results during the time I was coached by Colin, using the Preferred Reality model I have articulated in this book. Colin was able to help me explore my subconscious patterns that were negatively impacting my results, and to fully engage my superconscious to create a fantastic vision for myself, my business and my family.

Yet there are still certain areas I struggle with, not the least of which being my weight. I remember on more than one occasion having a conversation with Colin that went like this:

> *Richard:* 'Colin, I really want to lose weight.'
> *Colin:* 'No you don't.'
> *Richard:* 'Yes, I truly do.'
> *Colin:* 'No, you really don't.'
> *Richard:* 'Why do you say that, Colin?'
> *Colin:* 'Because if you did, you would stop stuffing food into your face!'

As I have said previously, it's not enough to just have a preferred reality, you also have to take action (like not continuing to stuff my face). So ask yourself, what do you truly want? What is the life you would love to lead, and what actions are you prepared to take in order to achieve it?

Your preferred reality

Start by writing down all the things you would love to have or accomplish in your life. If money was no obstacle, and your current commitments and lifestyle were no obstacle, what is the life you would truly choose for yourself?

A tool you can use to help with this is something I call the Lifestyle Wheel.

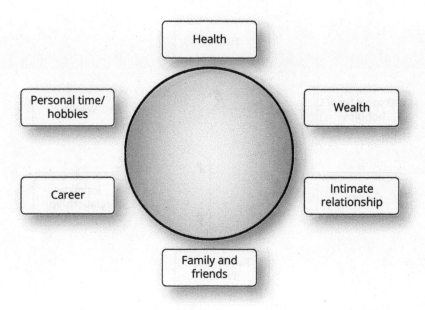

Imagine that the centre of the circle represents zero, and the outer edge of the circle represents 10. For each criterion, if 10 out of 10 represents your preferred reality, score yourself based on your opinion of your current reality, and then determine the action steps required to move you to your preferred reality.

If I was to do mine at the time of writing this book, it would look something like this:

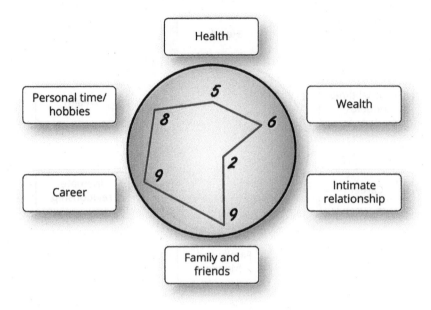

Let's break this down.

Health (five out of ten):

- Preferred reality: Under 90 kgs; completing 12,000+ steps per day; no chronic health issues.

- Current reality: 110 kgs; no consistent daily exercise; good health, considering.

- Action steps: Start working with a dietician and commit to their advice; get up early each day and walk for an hour; get an annual full medical done to ensure health remains good.

Wealth (six out of ten):

- Preferred reality: No debt; business delivering $x profit per annum; investment plan in place to retire comfortably by age 65.

- Current reality: Mortgage is $x; business loan is $x; business profit is 75 per cent of target; no investment plan in place.

- Action steps: Set specific goal date for full repayment of loans and commit to repayment schedule to achieve this; identify specific actions to increase revenue and decrease costs to hit business profit target and commit to these; engage a financial planner to help develop investment plan and commit to their advice.

Intimate relationship (two out of ten):

- Preferred reality: Actually I'm very happy being single at the moment, so even though I have rated it as two, you could say that it's actually a ten for me at the time of writing.

- Current reality: Single and loving it!

- Action steps: Have fun!

Family and friends (nine out of ten):

- Preferred reality: Have a large group of close friends and a great relationship with my kids and extended family.

- Current reality: Awesome, although you can never have too many friends, right?

- Action steps: Continue to invest in relationships, be happy and helpful, and enjoy the love.

Career (nine out of ten):

- Preferred reality: Do meaningful work; be of service; be regarded as a thought leader and trusted advisor; be well rewarded financially.

- Current reality: I love what I do; I believe I am truly helping people; and I'm being well rewarded.

- Action steps: Release a new podcast weekly; be a guest on someone else's podcast weekly; plan to write third book in 2025.

Personal time/hobbies (eight out of ten):

- Preferred reality: Meditate daily; sing and play in a band (I'm also a musician, and you can listen to my music on Spotify); cook and enjoy beautiful food.

- Current reality: Meditating most days although could be more consistent; haven't played in a band since COVID; am cooking and eating delicious food (perhaps a bit too much …).

- Action steps: Ensure daily meditation is in diary and prioritised; catch up with old bandmates and get a new project started (my last band was called the Big Love Jam Band); choose equally delicious but lower calorie meals to cook.

Anyway, you get the picture. This is a great habit to get into and review at least once a year. Put your action steps into a table, just like the one we did for Sam, the new Sales Manager. Ask someone to hold you accountable, preferably not an immediate family member or friend because they may have a bias for you to continue with your old, unproductive behaviour. For example, my family may still enjoy and want to encourage me to keep cooking gourmet, high-calorie meals (they are delicious).

You can even share your goals and actions with your team, to demonstrate you are 'walking the talk'. There's a strong push for leaders to be more vulnerable, so perhaps sharing your achievements and also your struggles is a great way of doing this (which is also why I have shared mine in this book). Just remember your virtue of prudence – be careful who you share your truth with. You have worked hard and deserve having a life you truly love. A big part of this is having employees who are making a meaningful contribution to you achieving what you want, and a boss or board who do the same. Utilising the Preferred Reality model across these relationships will help ensure that you and everyone involved in your life gets to achieve their full potential.

In this chapter, you have learned:

★ The Preferred Reality model is also a fantastic tool for setting and then holding yourself accountable to your own goals.

★ Take a holistic approach and include all elements of your life.

★ Engage with a coach or another trusted person to hold you accountable.

★ Live the life you would love to live – you deserve it.

Chapter 19

'Bon voyage': knowing how to say goodbye

'Bon voyage'

As much as this part of the book is about retaining top performers, one of the downsides to developing someone to achieve their highest potential is at some point they will probably leave. Your business may just not have the capacity to continue to offer someone ongoing career growth and/or increased remuneration.

We have already talked about hiring well and firing fast, so there's no need to rehash what to do with people who are either under-performing or a poor cultural fit. Manage these people stringently with KPIs (which can also cover soft skills, like ability to get on with the team), meet regularly, keep good notes, and move them towards either resignation or termination. Speak to an IR lawyer to make sure you are getting the best advice, at the time, around the specific situation. I've had to terminate two employees in the last five years and in both instances my IR lawyer made sure my process was beyond reproach. Susannah McAuliffe, your fees were definitely worth it.

Back in 2011, when Arete was only two years old, I met a young guy named Tim Wallis at a Property Council Christmas party. Having had a few drinks, we got into a conversation at the bar, largely about complete rubbish, however I really liked Tim and felt we had a great rapport. He was working at the time in a junior marketing communications role for an engineering company.

Even though Tim had never worked in the recruitment industry, the very next day I reached out to him and invited him for a meeting to discuss him joining Arete. He ended up working for me for over seven years, was a great employee, and we developed an excellent working relationship.

In 2018, Tim came to me and said he was keen to join a larger recruitment company where he could be part of a bigger, national team. As much as I wanted to retain him, I completely understood his motivation for finding a new job. I helped him in selecting which firms to approach and I proactively acted as his referee. He ended up securing a new role, where he has worked for the last five years. I note on his LinkedIn profile that he has now been promoted to a Director role. I couldn't be prouder of what he has achieved.

I was absolutely gutted when Tim left. Tim's resignation cost me a substantial amount of money and time in trying to replace him, and 'kissing a few frogs' along the way. It was absolutely the last thing I needed at the time.

I'm not ashamed to say that at Tim's going away lunch I cried, and not just a little. I cried a *lot*, including in the Uber on the way home (I'd had more than a few drinks). Tim had been an excellent employee, delivered fantastic results, and had also become a great colleague and trusted confidante. While we no longer see each other often, we still catch up occasionally, refer each other candidates, and have a strong and positive relationship.

My point is this. Good people are going to leave your business. Instead of being angry and bitter, make sure they leave feeling valued and appreciated. At the very least, you want them to remain a good advocate for you and your business in the future.

Plus, you never know, they may come back. Tim, just give me a call, mate, anytime …

In this chapter, you have learned:

★ All things must change – life is impermanent and so are your teams.

★ Good leaders develop their staff to achieve their highest potential, which can often (unfortunately) result in them moving on.

★ Remember your virtue of fortitude – wishing good fortune on others, as you also wish for yourself.

Chapter 20

We have reached the end

Congratulations on picking up this book and making the commitment to read it all the way through. Hopefully you now feel empowered to take better control of your own recruitment process; to not only hire top performers but also to retain them in your business.

The ongoing success of your business relies so much on your people. Having learned the methodology I have outlined in this book, you can now with confidence and excitement approach your recruitment and retention responsibilities.

If you delegate these responsibilities to members of your team, both line managers and/or HR or recruitment teams, you now have the knowledge to be able to hold them to account for delivering you excellent results. No longer will excuses like 'there's a war for talent' or 'the great resignation' be acceptable.

Let's do a quick recap

We've covered a lot, so let's do a quick recap.

You know that recruiting top performers starts by ensuring that you and your company have a fantastic brand as an Employer of Choice. Your LinkedIn profiles and company website play a pivotal role in presenting your brand in the marketplace.

With each new recruitment exercise, there are pros and cons of using external recruiters versus your own internal team. Each vacancy can be assessed at the time to determine the best course of action. Is it a confidential or a highly specialised role? Will it require headhunting to ensure success or will a more generic recruitment process for sourcing candidates be sufficient?

You understand how critical a great brief is to ensure success. If you want to employ people who have 'done it before, done it well, and are motivated to do it again', you need to be absolutely clear on what success looks like in the role.

You are sourcing candidates through referrals, advertisements and headhunting. These candidates must be treated with dignity and respect. Disgruntled applicants will not assist you in sustaining your brand as an Employer of Choice.

You are utilising Lou Adler's fantastic 'one question interview' technique, plus his 10-factor scorecard to elicit the best information to allow you to make an informed hiring decision. You are utilising his 11-factor assessment to understand a candidate's motivation for considering your role, in order to deal with any potential future counteroffers.

Your recruitment process is robust and includes psychometric testing and verification checks (if deemed appropriate), and reference checks (absolutely essential). You can negotiate great offers to close the deal and hire that fantastic person.

You are now onboarding new team members into a performance culture to set them up immediately for success. You are implementing the Preferred Reality model across your entire business and are comfortably and confidently finding that fine balance between love and accountability.

You are operating from a position of high integrity with your virtues intact and clearly demonstrated. You are the King, and not the Jester!

Plus you've perhaps had your eyes opened to some new perspectives around consciousness and the way the mind works (including your own).

Wow – what an awesome leader you are! Can I come and work for you? Seriously, I'm so impressed. As will be your incumbent team, your boss, other key stakeholders, plus anyone looking to join your business. You truly are an Employer of Choice. You can't help but achieve your full potential.

This book is a call to action. Take responsibility for developing your skills, so you are consistently hiring and retaining the very best talent. Take responsibility for living your preferred reality, the life that you would truly love to live.

Set yourself some large activity targets and make sure you fulfil them. No amount of knowledge is useful unless you put it to good use.

I really look forward to hearing your success stories. All the people who have implemented the information in this book have gone on to build great businesses, build great careers, and build amazing teams. I would love it if the next success story was yours.

Are you excited? I know I am.

I wish you all the very best in life.

Big love

Triggsy

Unlock the secrets to attracting and retaining top talent with Richard Triggs, author of *Winning the War for Talent.*

Discover innovative strategies and actionable insights that can transform your hiring process and elevate your organisation's success.

Find out how you can work directly with Richard in the following pages.

RICHARD TRIGGS
Author • Speaker • Advisor

Richard Does A Lot Of Things

In today's fiercely competitive business landscape, securing top talent is more crucial than ever. Richard Triggs, renowned author of *Winning the War for Talent*, offers a comprehensive suite of services designed to help your organisation master the art of talent acquisition and retention.

Through his in-depth training sessions, and insightful podcast, Richard provides innovative strategies and practical solutions tailored to your company's unique needs.

By leveraging Richard's expertise, you'll not only attract and retain the best professionals in your industry but also transform your overall approach to talent management.

★ ★ ★

The best way to find out more about how you can work with Richard is to visit www.richardtriggs.com.au

★ ★ ★

www.richardtriggs.com.au

TRAINING YOUR TEAM

In today's fiercely competitive business landscape, securing top talent is more crucial than ever. Richard Triggs, renowned author of *Winning the War for Talent*, offers unparalleled training designed to help your organisation master the art of talent acquisition and retention. Richard's expertise will guide you through innovative strategies and practical solutions tailored to your company's unique needs, ensuring you not only attract but also retain the best professionals in your industry.

By engaging Richard's training, your team will gain valuable insights into creating a compelling employer brand, optimising recruitment processes, and fostering a culture that keeps top performers motivated and loyal.

A Richard Triggs team training workshop could have a dramatic impact on the future of your organisation.

www.richardtriggs.com.au

MEDIA

Would you like to interview Richard Triggs?

Richard Triggs is an authority when it comes to both career development and recruitment. Both sides of the employment discussion have changed dramatically in recent years. His unique experience and thinking around this make him ideally suited for all media formats.

Some of the topics that Richard can commentate on include:

- Smashing your competition by hiring the best – on time, every time
- Turbo charge your career – how to accelerate your accession to the best c-suite and board roles available
- The recruitment industry is dead – the future of hiring
- Hiring for true diversity rather than just ticking a box
- The War for Talent (and other business myths)
- Life beyond the great resignation (and what this means for employers
- Career Mastery – a framework for achieving your full potential

To arrange an interview
with Richard Triggs
please email directly at
info@richardtriggs.com.au

www.richardtriggs.com.au

SPEAKER

Looking for a powerful, intelligent, and considered speaker for your next event?

Richard Triggs is the expert you need. With his finger on the pulse of executive employment, recruitment, and workforce dynamics, Richard delivers unique insights that are both informative and valuable. His "no nonsense" approach to career development emphasises personal responsibility in a rapidly changing world, offering strategies that benefit both individuals seeking career growth and organisations aiming to attract top talent.

Engage Richard Triggs to bring a fresh, impactful perspective to your event. His proven strategies and actionable advice resonate with audiences, driving real change and growth. The best way to get started is to have a preliminary discussion with Richard about your event and your goals. He will tailor his presentation to meet your specific needs and exceed your expectations. Contact Richard Triggs today to elevate your next event to a whole new level.

To find out more about having Richard as a speaker at your event please email info@richardtriggs.com.au

www.richardtriggs.com.au